THE RUSSIAN REVOLUTION
and
THE INDIAN FREEDOM STRUGGLE

THE RUSSIAN REVOLUTION
and
THE INDIAN FREEDOM STRUGGLE

From the Pages of History, A Vision for Future

Conceptualisation
S. Sudhakar Reddy

Editor
Jaya Mehta

Joshi-Adhikari Institute of Social Studies
(JAISS)

AAKAR

The Russian Revolution and the Indian Freedom Struggle
Edited by Jaya Mehta

First Published 2018
Reprinted 2020

ISBN 978-93-5002-580-2

Published by
AAKAR BOOKS
28 E Pocket IV, Mayur Vihar Phase I
Delhi 110 091, India
www.aakarbooks.com

Front Cover: Lenin stands in front of the troops sent to the Polish front. Moscow Sverdlov Square, May 5, 1920. Photographer unknown.

Cover Design: Archishman Raju and Ashutosh Singh Rajput

Printed at
Sapra Brothers, Noida

Contents

Part 3: Post-Independence Period

PREFACE
Pages from History: A Vision for the Future

We present a collection of articles that connect two great world revolutionary movements, the Russian Revolution and the Indian anti-colonial struggle. The articles are not meant to be academic publications and should not be read as such. Rather, they are reflections of the thinking and practice of the leadership of the Communist Party of India, how it was influenced by the ideas of the Russian Revolution and at the same time, had to adapt to local conditions in its struggle against British rule in India. In many of the articles, we have added boxes highlighting one particular concept or figure mentioned.

We have divided the book into three parts. The first part gives a theoretical framework to the understanding of the Russian Revolution and the anti-colonial struggle. The second part covers the pre-independence period of the relationship between the freedom struggle and the Russian Revolution. The third part is on the post-independence period and the relationship between independent India and the Soviet Union. Some of the articles also cover world situation after dismantling of Soviet Union.

Since the articles have not been written for the purpose of this publication, they naturally do not fit neatly into such a division so this is only a rough categorisation. All the articles, with the exception of Lenin and M.N. Roy's theses and the article by Prabhat

Patnaik, are from *New Age*, the central organ of the Communist Party of India. The articles have been written at different points of time which should be kept in mind when reading them.

This collection is being released in honour of the 100th anniversary of the Russian Revolution and we begin the collection with a message by Com. S. Sudhakar Reddy, General Secretary of the Communist Party of India. We hope that these articles will not only serve as a reminder of an era of mass movements, but will also offer insight into the thinking and practice of the leadership of the Communist Party of India and offer direction in an age of global crisis of world capitalism.

The book was conceptualised by Comrade S. Sudhakar Reddy. He thought that on the occasion of the centenary year of the October Revolution, its impact on India should be looked at by compiling the articles written on this theme by our leaders at various stages of development of free India.

Comrade Balakrisna Nair (Balan) dug out around sixty articles from CPI's central organ *New Age*. Com. Sudhakar Reddy went through the preliminary list and selected the articles which would give wide enough coverage. Articles were organised and supplemented by introductions and boxes by Archishman Raju, Vineet Tiwari, Dr. C. Sadasiva, Nandita Chaturvedi, Vivek Sharma and Sourav Banerjee.

Valuable help in this exercise was offered by Dr. Koninika Ray, Kritika and Anuja Rajan. Ashutosh Singh Rajput helped design the covers. The book layout and design is done by Dhruva Narayan of JANAM Foundation.

Jaya Mehta

Carry Forward the Message of Great October Socialist Revolution

S. Sudhakar Reddy

November 7, 2016, marks the beginning of the hundredth year of the Great October Socialist Revolution. Peace-loving progressive forces around the world, under the banner of the communist and workers parties, will be celebrating its triumphant and glorious march through the pages of history. In India too, the day will be observed throughout the country. The national executive of our party has decided to observe a year-long celebration of the day beginning with this November 7.

The hundred years since 1917 have been years of hard toil and struggle, of great achievement and victory of unsurpassed heroism and valour for the forces of revolution. In the land of Lenin and in the world arena, these have been years of upholding the rights of the oppressed and the exploited for emancipation from all kinds of

---

This message by Comrade S. Sudhakar Reddy, General Secretary, Communist Party of India, was delivered on the occasion of the beginning of the centenary celebrations of the Great October Revolution.

exploitation and of a march towards an egalitarian society. The banner of the Great October Socialist Revolution is today the banner of all those who stand for end to imperialism and capitalism, to hunger and exploitation, against reactionary Right's concerted attempts to turn back the clock of human progress and for man's well being and progress.

The birth of the first socialist state in 1917 no doubt had changed the entire face of the earth. It was the most significant event of the last century heralding a new era and a new destiny for mankind. It overthrew the exploitative Czarist Empire in Russia and brought into existence a new society based upon the equality of man and power of the working class. It breached the walls of world imperialism for the first time in history and struck a major blow to its might, provoking the forces of world imperialism to unleash all kinds of intimidation, boycott and surveillance against the new born state. Despite all attempts to tarnish the birth of the first socialist state, the success of the revolution brought inspiration for the toiling people all over the world and hopes of a new life. The people of Asia, Africa and Latin America groaning under the yoke of colonialism found a new ally in the form of a whole recognised state.

In the decades that followed October Revolution, the people of the erstwhile Soviet Union made tremendous progress in all fields of human endeavour. The living standards of all sections rose to a new height. Under the leadership of the Communist Party of Soviet Union, the Soviet people literally crossed new frontiers in social and economic development and marched towards "to each according to his needs" guaranteeing rights to the people that are even today unthinkable in any other society. No wonder such advancement of Soviet society irked the forces of exploitation further. Today when once again world imperialism after its failure to lead a uni-polar world is attempting to crush the forces of peace, social progress and human development, it must be noted here that ever since Lenin issued the 'Decree of Peace' – the very first step taken by the young socialist state – the people of the Soviet Union have been fighting for peace and against the dark forces of war and carnage. Their deciding role in crushing the Hitlerite hordes in the Second World War, their indomitable courage and heroism saved mankind from the terror of Nazi domination. It led to the birth of a new alternative – the world socialist system – that gave unparalleled impetus to the national liberation movements in the colonial countries. As a result more than a hundred newly freed nations emerged on the world scene.

The Great October Revolution stood firmly against imperialism and the forces of war and plunder, of exploitation and oppression and as a friend indeed of the suffering people and subjugated nations, upholding the cause of national liberation movements, allying with anti-imperialist and progressive forces. Our own freedom struggle has drawn inspiration and strength from the October Revolution and from the success of the first socialist state. The bonds that were forged between the victorious revolution in Russia and our national liberation movement grew stronger and achieved a new content after the country achieved independence. It blossomed into many-sided co-operation in the fields of economy, trade, agriculture, education, scientific research, sports, culture etc.

In today's India when the right wing forces are trying their best to undo all that we have achieved since our independence, it must be borne in mind that the Soviet assistance has provided powerful weapons for our struggle for economic self-reliance and for independent economic development against feudalism, monopoly and neo-colonialism. Not only in economic matters but on political issues also the Soviet Union has stood by India, be it on the issue of Kashmir, Goa or Bangladesh. The abiding friendship and co-operation for mutual benefit between India and Soviet Union have been exemplified in the Indo-Soviet Treaty of Friendship and Cooperation.

The Great October Revolution will definitely continue to shine as the lodestar for the toiling people in their onward march for all the times to come. It underlines the everlasting validity of the principles of Marxism-Leninism and proletarian internationalism. It provides the impetus to the oppressed and the exploited to fight till their goal is reached. On this historic day we affirm our pledge to carry forward the banner of the Great October Socialist Revolution, of Marxism-Leninism, of proletarian internationalism and fight against the right wing forces in the best traditions of the world communist movement.

Long Live the October Revolution!

Part 1

Theoretical Foundations

"The Worker and Kolkhoz woman"
The sculpture was made of Stainless steel by the famous Russian sculptor Vera Mukhina for the Paris World Fair in 1937. It was later shifted to Moscow. It was 24.5 metres (78 feet) high and put on a pedestal of 10 metres giving it a total height of 34.5 metres. In 2009, the sculpture was restored at an elevated pedestal of 34.5 metres giving it a total height of 60 metres.

Introduction (Part 1)

Lenin wrote the book '*Imperialism, the Highest Stage of Capitalism*' which was published in 1917. This was the period of the First World War. Lenin argued that the First World War was an intra-imperialist war whose purpose was to partition and re-partition the colonies and divide them between imperialist countries.

The intra-imperialist war brought loss of innocent lives and enormous suffering, but it created space for the revolutionary agenda. Lenin gave a call to the working masses – Instead of fighting with your fellow workers across the trenches, turn your guns inwards. Transform the imperialist war into civil war to overthrow the capitalist ruling class and the monarchy.

The Socialist Revolution in Russia initiated an unending debate regarding revolution and the stage of capitalist development.

The articles by R. Palme Dutt and Prabhat Patnaik explain the October Revolution in a theoretical conceptual frame based on Marxist-Leninist coordinates. R.P. Dutt's article talks of the specific characteristic of the proletariat of Russia and the revolutionary party which was dynamic and focused. Prabhat Patnaik talks at length about worker-peasant alliance and its importance in the revolutionary agenda. Both articles elaborate the theoretical perspective of the October Revolution with reference to the world revolutionary project.

The Communist movement has had three Internationals. The first two were founded and based primarily in Europe. The First International formed in 1864 had Karl Marx, Engels, Bakunin and others in it. It did not survive for very long because of disagreement between socialists and anarchists. The Second International was formed in 1889 and was explicitly a socialist International including figures like Lenin and Karl Kautsky. The Second International collapsed in the middle of the First World War because with the exception of Lenin and his supporters, its members refused to take a principled stand against the war. The Third International or the Communist International formed in 1919 by Lenin after the Russian Revolution was explicitly against imperialist wars and for peace.

It is well known that after the advent of the Russian Revolution, the leaders were looking towards Germany in the hope that an advanced capitalist country would also undergo a revolution. However, a revolution failed to happen, and the revolutionary wing of the German socialists was defeated. This was when Lenin decided to rethink the trajectory of world revolution. This is also when M.N. Roy attended the Second Congress of the Communist International in July-August 1920. Lenin had already been thinking and preparing a thesis on the national and colonial question. He argued in his thesis that Russia could no longer look to the West, but must look towards the anti-colonial struggles in the East. He then invited criticisms and comments. M.N. Roy was one of the attendees who responded to the request and prepared a supplementary thesis on the national and colonial question. M.N. Roy argued, like Rosa Luxemburg had in her book on *The Accumulation of Capital*, that European capital was able to survive because of the continued control over colonial markets. That, without the super-exploitation of labour in the colonies, European capital would "have collapsed under its own weight". M.N. Roy went further to say that the

European working class could not overthrow the capitalist order, unless the colonies were free and no longer served as a market for imperialism. That is, he argued that Europe could not be free unless Africa and Asia were free. Finally, Roy brought out a distinction between the "bourgeois democratic movement" and the struggle of the "propertyless peasants". He said that the Communist International should only support the latter. Lenin disagreed and thought that the primary enemy was British imperialism against which many different social forces would have to come together in a united front. He said that the communists in India should remain independent but must support the bourgeois-democratic movement against British imperialism. It is worth noting that Virendranath Chattopadhyaya (Chatto) disagreed with Roy and also felt that British imperialism was the primary enemy. Finally, an agreement was reached and it was decided that the Communist International would support any "national revolutionary movement". Both Lenin's thesis and Roy's supplementary thesis were adopted by the Communist International. This period in history is very important because it sets the basis for the policy of the Soviet Union towards world revolution. They offered generous support to liberation movements in Africa and Asia.

Along with the articles of R.P. Dutt and Prabhat Patnaik, we also include Lenin's "Draft Theses on Colonial and National Question" and the supplementary theses of M.N. Roy in this section.

Delegates to the Second Congress of the Communist International at the Uritsky Palace in Petrograd. Lenin is in front corner, Maxim Gorky is just behind him and M.N. Roy is in the centre, tall man in coat and tie, 1920.

1

The Revolution of All Revolutions

R. Palme Dutt

Modern history is the history of revolutions. Every major modern state is founded on a revolution. The most ultra-conservatives today claim to be the true disciples of a preceding revolution in order to denounce the living revolution in their midst. The most hidebound constitutionalists in Britain boast of their fidelity to the principles of what they are pleased to call the Glorious Revolution. The most viciously reactionary ladies of property in the United States call themselves the Daughters of the American Revolution. All the great revolutions which have constituted the foundations of the modern states have been international in their significance.

The English seventeenth century revolution – the Great Revolution, not the miscalled 'Glorious Revolution', which was a counter-revolutionary restoration – led the way to the modern world; and the Russian Ambassador was withdrawn in protest at the regicide nation, defended by the inspired pen of Milton, England's poet who had no fear to be 'committed'. The American eighteenth century revolution carried forward the advance; and the Englishman, Thomas Paine, hero of the American Revolution and Deputy for Calais, became the living link of the American and

French revolutions. The French Revolution illuminated the whole nineteenth century, until the Paris Commune foreshadowed the future victory of the working class. But all these preceding victorious revolutions, which established the modern capitalist states, while claiming each in turn to represent the victory of humanity, equality and freedom, represented in fact the victory of a class without ending the class basis of society.

The October Revolution, the Russian socialist revolution of 1917, eclipsed all the preceding revolutions, not only in its range and international impact, but in its essential character that, by bringing the victory of the last exploited class, the working class, it represented victory over the old class society, and opened the path to the new classless society of socialism advancing to communism. Fifty years have now passed since the victory of the October Revolution. The world transformation which it opened continues to extend.

Why revolution first in Russia?

Why did the socialist revolution begin in Russia? This question is worth posing at the outset, because it is vital for the understanding of the international significance of the October Revolution. The legend is sedulously spread to trap the unwary that Marx and all socialists expected the revolution to begin in the most advanced capitalist countries of Western Europe. Therefore, the conclusion is drawn, the occurring of the socialist revolution in such a backward country as Russia, with its heavy feudal survivals, weak economic development, limited working class and overwhelming peasant majority, was either impermissible as contrary to Marxism (Kautsky's view), or, in the more favoured modern version, a complete disproof of the dogmatic assumption and illusion of Marxism.

On the foundation of this false premise a whole further argument is carried forward concerning the extension of the socialist revolution since 1945 to a series of countries in Asia or the less developed capitalist countries of Eastern Europe, to present the grand conclusion that Marxism or communism is only applicable to backwards countries, but is wholly inapplicable to the advanced capitalist countries of Western Europe and North America. This current fashionable line of argument represents a remarkable inversion on the part of the opponents of Marxism.

The early Russian Marxists had attempted ceaselessly to combat the allegation that Marxism was of course applicable to advanced West European capitalist countries, but not to a peasant country like Russia. Now the exact opposite has become the favourite doctrine of the opponents of Marxism. There is, however, consistency in this apparent complete somersault and contradiction. The consistency is that any argument is valid so long as it can prove that Marxism cannot apply to the speaker's own country.

This whole vast theoretical construction is based on simple ignorance of what Marx said. Up to 1848 Marx and Engels did expect the socialist revolution to develop from the victory of the democratic revolution in the most advanced capitalist region of Western Europe. They proclaimed this in the Communist Manifesto. Even here it is worth noting that they anticipated the first victory of the socialist revolution, not in the most advanced capitalist country, England, but in the country with a weaker economy and heavy feudal survivals, Germany, because they believed that the bourgeois revolution in Germany will be but the prelude to an immediately following proletarian revolution.

Here, in this premature expectation, the principle of looking, not to the single most advanced capitalist country in isolation as the starting point, but to the key focus of contradictions in the whole capitalist network, is already foreshadowed. This is the principle which Marx and Engels in their later writings correctly and explicitly transferred to Russia. After the defeat of the 1848 revolution, Marx and Engels separated themselves from the anticipations of the other exiles looking for a speedy resumption of the revolution in Germany or Western Europe. Engels wrote plainly in 1895 (in his Preface to Marx's 'Class Struggles' in French), with regard to the 1848 anticipations of impending socialist revolution in

Western Europe: 'History has proved us and all who thought like us, wrong'.

From the Eighteen-Fifties Marx was turning attention to the world development of capitalism; the prospective displacement of British economic supremacy by the United States; the significance of the opening up of China and Japan; the new role of the Pacific; he was writing his masterly series of studies on the perspective in India; he was predicting the future victory of an independent India and of the Chinese republic. And it was in this context of the world development of capitalism that he was declaring already in 1858, in a letter to Engels, that the perspective of the socialist revolution needed henceforth to be seen in terms of world capitalism rather than in 'this little corner' of Europe.

Carrying forward this line of thought, from the opening of the last quarter of the nineteenth century, Marx and Engels specifically referred to Russia as 'the vanguard of revolutionary action in Europe'; 'this time the revolution will begin in the East'. Once again the principle was followed of seeing the capitalist network as a whole, now in terms of world capitalism, and looking to the central focus of contradictions where the revolution could begin, initially as a bourgeois democratic revolution which could rapidly be carried forward to a proletarian revolution. That the subjective conditions were gathering for this development was indicated by the fact that the first translation of Marx's *Capital* was the Russian translation in 1872 (Fourteen years before the English translation), and the most intelligent perceptive review of it was a Russian review which Marx quoted at length with warm appreciation in his Preface to the Second Edition in 1873.

Focus of contradictions

That the expectation of the future role of Russia as the vanguard of the revolution was no random expectation was illustrated by the remarkable prediction of Engels in 1888 with regard to the prospect of the European war of 1914, when he said that there would be no triumphal marched on Paris or Berlin, but 'a war of positions on the French Frontier' (i.e. trench warfare), and that there would then follow 'a revolution in Petersburg' which would transform the situation. And now the October Revolution, which is thus the triumphant vindication of the insights and predictions, as well as of the class analysis and strategic and tactical lines of Marxism, is coolly presented by all the conventional academic, radio and big press asses as the supposed disproof of Marxism.

But the significance of Russia as the focus of all the contradictions of imperialism in the midst of the world war in 1917 would not be enough to explain the victory of the socialist revolution if there were not the class forces and political leadership to make that victory possible. Marxism taught that decisive role of the industrial working class, not as the majority of the population (Britain is the only country where the industrial working class has been an absolute majority of the population), but as the only consistent revolutionary force, whose interest are directly opposed to those of the exploiters and owners of the means of production: the only force capable from the conditions of their exploitation under capitalism to achieve solidarity and large-scale organisation; and therefore capable of leading all the varied and fluctuating and weakly organised masses of all exploited sections of the populations, especially the peasantry, as also the artisans, handicraftsmen, small traders, urban petty bourgeoisie and intelligentsia, to a common united victory against the landlords and big capitalists. This truth of Marxism, which remains cardinal also today in all the many new conditions arising, was brilliantly demonstrated by the whole process of the 1917 revolution in Russia.

The notion commonly expressed by the asses that, because the old Russia was economically backward and a predominantly peasant country, therefore the Russian working class was a tiny backward minority incapable of playing a significant role, and the October Revolution was made by the subjective will of Lenin and a handful of Bolshevik fanatics, is based on simple ignorance. Modern machine industry in Russia was limited in extent and mainly owned by foreign capitalists. By the end of the nineteenth century the industrial proletariat numbered 2.7 million. But the industry that did exist represented a higher level of large-scale enterprise than in any of the most advanced industrial countries. Nearly half the industrial workers (48.3 per cent) were concentrated in enterprises employing over 500 workers.

This represented a higher proportion of the industrial workers in large-scale enterprises than in Germany, Britain or the United States. At the same time the exploitation was intense. Hence a unique situation arose. This Russian industrial proletariat had a record without equal over the preceding two decades of active struggle mass strike, political strike and tenacious maintenance of organisation in face of illegality, police terror and armed violence. Following the 1905 revolution the conception of the mass strike, drawn from Russian experience, became the centre of all European socialist discussion.

No wonder Kautsky already in 1902, writing then as the recognised spokesman of Marxism, reached the same conclusion as Marx and Engels had previously done, that 'the revolutionary centre is shifting from the West to the East. The new century opens with events which suggest the idea that we are approaching a further shift of the revolutionary centre, namely, to Russia. (Kautsky in *Iskra*, March 10, 1902).

This advanced vanguard role of the Russian working class, thus recognised by the spokesmen of the international working class movement from the beginning of the twentieth century, could not have been achieved, however intense the exploitation, and however heroic the struggle, if that struggle had not been combined with the guiding strength, sense of direction and indomitable will of revolutionary Marxist political consciousness of the most militant class-conscious workers, which found expression in the Marxist party, the party based on the teachings of Marx and Lenin, the Bolshevik party.

Individual Heroism to Mass Action

Here also the unique situation occurred that the highest revolutionary tradition of the Russian nineteenth century revolutionary intelligentsia, who had groped for a solution through individual heroism or through utopian exaltation of the village community as the expression of 'the people' had, through the guidance of Marxism won the most progressive sections and found the path of unity with the organisation of the industrial working class to create thereby the invincible leading force which made possible the victory of the Russian Revolution and eventually of the socialist revolution.

This was the key to victory which found the path forward for the world. The experience of fifty years has abundantly confirmed the truth of this. Socialism has been achieved only in those countries where there has been the leadership of a Marxist-Leninist party. All the supposedly alternative non-Marxist paths to socialism, represented during these fifty years by the anti-communist social-democratic organisations, have completely failed to end capitalism or wrest the means of production out of the hands of the big monopolists, and have usually ended up in disgraceful coalitions with the bankers and big monopolists against the working class.

Herein lies the universal international significance of the October Revolution, however varied the concrete conditions and consequent particular tactical forms within each country. And it is just this burning truth, the key to victory in every country. The indispensable role of the political party of the most advanced sections of the working class on the basis of Marxism-Leninism, which all the learned lecturers are most concerned to conceal and deny in their versions of 1917. Instead, they try to peddle the infantile historical theories of the single-handed 'great man' as the maker of history, and present the picture of Lenin as the 'ruthless strong man' who 'imposed his will' on the 'inert Russian masses accustomed only to authoritarian rule' and with the aid of a handful of confederates 'seized power' and made himself 'dictator'.

The clown who posed as a historian in a television series on 1917 declared that the Bolsheviks had no part in the February Revolution which overthrew the Czar, and that their party at that time was insignificant, and scarcely anyone had heard of it. The ridiculousness of this declaration should be seen in the background that the Cambridge Modern History, published in 1910, had devoted in its Russian section two pages to the significance of Lenin and the Bolsheviks. Already before 1914, Lenin was able to claim with incontestable facts that Bolshevik Party had 'brought about the unity of Four-Fifths of the class-conscious workers of Russia. About forty thousand workers had been buying *Pravda*; far more read it. In the October 1912 elections to the Duma the Bolsheviks won all the six seats reserved for the workers. On the very eve of the war in July 1914 the political strike movement had reached such heights, moving towards revolutionary situation, that the barricades were up in Petersburg.

It is true that under the blows of the intensified war repression all the main leaders of the Bolshevik Party were struck down, arrested, imprisoned, exiled in Siberia or already in emigration. But the extreme war repression could not kill the party. The Petersburg Committee was reconstituted no less than thirty times during the war.

It was the Petersburg committee (alongside the parallel activities of Bolshevik Party committees in the other main towns) which was in the forefront of the leadership in the organisation of the extending strike movement and illegal demonstrations during the war years. Culminating in the rising tempo of the first ten weeks of 1917; the Putilov strike (with 150 Bolshevik members in the works) in the beginning of March 1917; the party call for solidarity strikes from the other factories; the organisation of International Women's Day on March 8; the party call to the soldiers to fraternise with the workers; and so the overwhelming irresistible advance of the revolutionary mass movements which compelled the downfall of czarism and took by surprise the Duma leaders and moderate pro-war socialist leaders who to the last were trying to negotiate a compromise with the czarist regime. Thus the February Revolution was the first stage of the Bolshevik revolution.

If at the moment of the victory of this first stage of the mass revolution the Duma bourgeois leaders and their 'moderate' socialist associates were able to proclaim themselves the new government in the name of a revolution in which they had in fact no share, and if the Bolsheviks who had in fact been the political leaders in the mass revolutionary upsurge bringing down czarism, found themselves at first in a minority in the Soviets, this was because the very success of the revolution had awakened new scores and scores of millions to active political life, who had no previous political experience.

Therefore the Bolsheviks had to undertake anew with infinite patience, tenacity and flexibility a vast work of explanations, mass agitation and propaganda, with demonstration in practical experience of the ruinous consequences of reactionary policies masquerading under 'socialist labels', until at last they had won the majority in the Soviets, in trade union representation, in the key army units, as well as in significant municipal elections, and thereby were able to fulfil their task of leadership for the conquest of power by the working class uniting the overwhelming majority of the people in the most bloodless revolution in history.

But the violence? Destruction of freedom? Tyranny? Terror? The excesses during the period of Stalin's later leadership? Let us be clear a little on the facts of the struggle between revolution and counter revolution, and the responsibility for violence. And let us confine our testimony to enemy witnesses.

Kerensky's show was fake

First, on the character of the 'democracy' of Kerensky which the Bolshevik Revolution overthrew. The 'democratic methods' of Kerensky included the suppression of the Finnish parliament, which had the first socialist absolute parliamentary majority in history and demanded independence (it was the Bolsheviks who gave Finland independence) the suppression of newspapers, prohibition of meetings and arrest of political opponents (Lenin had to be in hiding by party decision to escape arrest) such that the British imperialist historian Sir John Mayanard described Kerensky's regime as a 'virtual dictatorship' (*The Russian Peasant*, p. 73). The intrigues of Kerensky with General Kornilov and his savage decision of marching on Petrograd would have brought victory to a military counter-revolution had not the Bolsheviks defeated the coup and saved the Russian people.

Second, the character of the Bolshevik revolution as a victory of freedom, not only in the sense of ending the domination of the landlords and capitalists, but directly as a victory of the popular masses through the most democratic organs yet evolved in history, the Soviets, and therefore as involving the minimum bloodshed known in any great revolutions. Major-General Sir Alfred Knox, hostile to the Bolsheviks, recorded that the total number of casualties caused by the revolutions in the capital Petrograd, was about ten (*With the Russian Army*, Vol. 2, p.711). An underestimate of all the casualties involved, but sufficient evidence of the impression created on a hostile observer of the overwhelming popular support of the revolution. One of the earliest decrees was the abolition of capital punishment; the opposition parties and press continued unmolested; the czarist generals were released and only asked to give their word of honour not to take up arms against the people - which, as soon as they got away, they promptly did, financed and armed by the Western powers.

In his revealing Memories of a British Agent, Sir Robert Bruce Lockhart, Head of the British Mission in Russia at the time, from whose office Captain Reilly and the rest organised their infamous murder plots, although Lockhart has denied complicity ("I lacked the moral courage to resign".) has given this testimony on the early days of the Bolshevik revolution:

There was no terror. The anti-Bolshevik newspapers continued to appear and to attack the Bolshevik policy with violent abuse. I mention this comparative tolerance of the Bolsheviks because the cruelties which followed later were the result of the intensification of the civil war. For the intensification of that bloody struggle Allied intervention was largely responsible.

White Terror was effectively met

Lockhart has told the truth. It was the Western imperialist powers and their agents, the bandit White Guard General whom they financed and armed, the assassination plots they organised, the White Terror they let lose wherever they could reach, which finally led to the counter-organisation of the Red Terror for a short period, the formation of the Cheka, and the stringent measures for the protection of the revolution. Bourgeois history always sheds noisy tears over the upper-class victims of revolutions, but slides over the far more numerous victims of counter-revolution. Conventional textbooks proclaim aloud the horror of the 'September Massacres' of the French Revolution, killing six hundred, but pass quickly over the thirty thousand done to death in the suppression of the Commune or the thirty thousand dying in the camps of the White Terror in Finland.

Marx long ago said that White Terror can only be met and mastered by Red Terror. Lenin never ceased to pour scorn on the hypocrisy of the spokesmen of Western imperialism who could slaughter ten million in their World War and then raise an outcry over the victims of revolution.

After the wars of intervention had failed, and the Soviet people hoped for peace, Western imperialists built up the even more monstrous military and terrorist machine to Nazism to strangle the revolution and subjugate the Soviet Union. This menace raised the struggle to new heights. Nazism sought to penetrate every country with its Fifth Column and openly proclaimed the aim to invade and enslave the Soviet Union. The Soviet people had to face a superhuman task to arm to confront the most powerful military machine ever known, before which every other European army was soon to go down, and to defeat enemy penetration.

In the course of successfully meeting this ordeal, dangerous and harmful excesses were committed by security organs under direct control of the implacable leader of the revolution, Stalin, so that the blows struck down not only enemy agents, but many brave and honest revolutionaries. Nevertheless, however heavy the cost, the superhuman task was accomplished. Nazism, which built its fifth Column in every other European country, could build none in the Soviet Union. There was no quisling in the Soviet Union. The Nazi armies were smashed. Humanity was saved.

In all the holocaust of human suffering which has accompanied this era of the downfall of a dying social order and the titanic struggles of humanity advancing to a new society, let us never forget where the heaviest responsibility for all this suffering, for all the millions of needless deaths and destruction lies. It lies with the old social order' which had already spread its colonial barbarism over all the continents of the world, exterminating whole human races. And which in its culminating convulsions has let loose two world wars with fifty million killed, world economic crisis without equal, the horrors of fascism and the gas chambers, the atom bomb, Hiroshima and Nagasaki, and now Vietnam.

Let us also not forget, when there is sometimes a tendency for some socialists in the west to lecture the Soviet people from the imaginary vantage point of a supposed moral superiority, our responsibility to the working class and socialist movement in Western Europe and the Unites States. The First World War was the signal of the general crisis of capitalism proclaiming the ripeness of the material conditions and the urgency of the socialist revolution in all developed capitalist countries. All the socialist parties, also the Labour Party, have pledged themselves to this task in the event of the outbreak of the impending European war.

The Russian workers alone of the leading parties kept their pledge. The majority leaders in Western and Central Europe broke their pledge and joined in hounding on the fratricidal conflict. Had the powerfully organised working class of Western and Central Europe united with the Russian working class in the victory of the socialist revolution, the path would have been easier. There would have been no world economic crisis, no fascism, and no Second World War. We would have been speeding forward in the common task of construction in a united socialist Europe alongside the liberated peoples of the former colonial countries. The Soviet people, the pioneers, had to pay the heaviest price in blood and tears for our failure.

The October Revolution has opened the new world era. All the change in the balance of the world, all the advance of human liberation that has been achieved, the extension of socialism among one third of mankind, the victories of national liberation bringing in view the approaching downfall of colonialism, the relegation of imperialism to a minority sector of the world, the desperate attempts of the rulers in the remaining imperialist countries to emulate belatedly the social achievements of the socialist countries – all this stems from the October Revolution.

The strength of the Soviet Union is the bulwark which has made it possible for even small countries to defy imperialism where before 1917 every colonial revolt was crushed without exception. The aid of the Soviet Union has opened new paths of non-capitalist reconstruction for the newly independent countries. The peace policy of the Soviet Union combined with vigilant armed strength, has held at bay the snarling dogs of the imperialist cold war and former noisily proclaimed plans for the destruction of communism, until by this year we have held off the threat of a third world war for a longer period than that which elapsed between the first two world wars, and can still prevent its outbreak by the united mobilisation of the peoples.

But the dangers are still grave. The United States' barbarous war of aggression is still expending against the people of Vietnam. In the Middle East the aggressor demands the right of the conqueror to hold on to the fruits of aggression in defiance of the United Nations. In Southern Africa the heroic freedom fighters of the alliance of the African National Congress and the Zimbabwe

African People's Union, in association with the fighters in Mozambique and Angola, are confronting the combined armed forces of the South Africa and Rhodesian racialists. In face of this open aggression of the armed forces of a foreign power invading what is still a British territory, to sustain an illegal regime the British Labour Government has shamefully entered into urgent confabulation with the Foreign Minister of the invading power and with the illegal regime in order to pull off a deal at the expense of the African liberation struggle.

In Britain the Scarborough Labour Conference has demonstrated the bankruptcy of Labour reformism to tackle the problems raised by the deepening crisis of British imperialism, and the urgent necessity for the Left to achieve the strength, clarity and unity essential in order to carry through the basic changes of policy which are required. This great fiftieth anniversary is not only the occasion to celebrate the achievements during this half century. It is also the call to action for the far-reaching still unfinished tasks which lie before us.

(New Age Weekly, November 5, 1967)

2

The Theoretical Significance of the October Revolution

Prabhat Patnaik

The October Revolution brought about a revolutionary change in the conception of revolution itself. All revolutions thenceforth, including the October Revolution itself, were to be located within this new conceptual universe. Prior to the October Revolution, socialism had been seen as the revolutionary project exclusively of the proletariat, which could be attempted where the proletariat had come into being as a major political force, and where therefore the polarisation of society between the bourgeoisie and the proletariat had been carried far enough. Socialism in short was seen as the project of the proletariat in the advanced capitalist countries. Marx and Engels had of course seen the possibilities of revolution in what we would today call the countries of the periphery, like India and Egypt; but the nature of such revolutions in the periphery and their connections with the project of socialism had remained undefined.

The October Revolution changed all that. It saw the revolutionary project within each country as part of that country's transition in phases towards socialism; it saw the revolutionary projects of the different countries as inter-linked, and constituting merely the different moments in an overall worldwide transition to socialism; and correspondingly it saw the revolutionary project within particular countries as being sustained by worker-peasant alliances (together with other oppressed classes) led by the proletariat, with the latter's leadership being necessary condition for a successful transition to socialism. This last perception was clearly expressed in Lenin's call to set up "Soviets of the working people" (as distinct from the working class) in oppressed and colonised countries.

This change in the conceptual understanding of the revolution arose not from any arbitrary or ad hoc or fanciful thinking, but from the material reality of imperialism. Imperialism had not only knit together the entire world, but was characterised by periodic attempts by rival powers to re-partition an already partitioned world through wars, in a situation marked by inter-imperialist rivalry. Such wars of course brought enormous suffering; but they also helped the development of a revolutionary consciousness, not just among the workers in advanced capitalist countries who were asked to fight their fellow workers across the trenches for enhancing the "economic territories" at the command of "their" respective monopoly combines, but to the working people of the oppressed countries as well, who served as cannon-fodder in such wars.

This conceptual change in the vision of revolution did not come all at once. The fact that in countries coming late to capitalism, the bourgeoisie could not carry the democratic revolution against the feudal order to its completion, since it feared that any attack on feudal property could rebound into an attack on bourgeois property, had already been noted by Lenin and the Bolsheviks earlier. The peasants' desire for freedom from the feudal yoke, they saw, could not be fulfilled by the praxis of the bourgeoisie; it required a revolution which only the proletariat could lead. This made the peasantry an ally of the proletariat in the democratic revolution, and it therefore made the democratic revolution itself a stage in the process of transition to socialism, during which the precise allies of the proletariat would of course keep changing.

This idea of a new kind of democratic revolution based on a worker-peasant alliance, where the working class would not remain content with merely completing the anti-feudal tasks of such a revolution but would carry the revolution forward to socialism, with its allies changing along the way, had found theoretical expression in Lenin's "Two Tactics of Social Democracy in the Democratic Revolution" and had been practically incorporated into the programme of the Bolsheviks which visualised a "Revolutionary Democratic Dictatorship of Workers and Peasants".

What this entailed was a fundamental change in the attitude to the peasantry; but this change again was an outcome not simply of a different way of thinking, but of a different material reality. A democratic revolution of the kind that the French Revolution had been, where the bourgeoisie had played the leadership role and had destroyed feudal property and redistributed land to the peasants, was no longer possible in countries arriving late on the scene of bourgeois development. Correspondingly therefore, the relationship between the three classes, the bourgeoisie, the working class and the peasantry, had to be different in the new context from what it had been in the old context.

Earlier, the fact of the bourgeoisie having led the democratic revolution that brought landownership to the peasantry had made possible a unity of the bourgeoisie and the peasantry against the working class. It is this which had defeated the Paris Commune, with Adolphe Thiers putting the fear into the minds of the French peasants that any attack on bourgeois property would also entail an attack on peasant property. But, now, in countries like Russia there was an altogether new situation: because of the bourgeoisie's inability to attack feudal property, the proletariat had the historic opportunity to form an alliance with the peasantry, which via a democratic revolution, would lead on to socialism.

Many have interpreted this shift in the attitude to the peasantry on the part of the Marxists wrongly. They have argued that Marxism before the October Revolution had been hostile to the peasantry, while the October Revolution signified an overcoming of this hostility. This is not true: the Russian Marxists' changed attitude to the peasantry was not a mere matter of an altered attitude; it too was based on a change in the material reality, namely the bourgeoisie's incapacity to carry out the anti-feudal democratic revolution in the new situation.

It is the historic achievement of Lenin and the Bolsheviks that they recognised this change in material reality. In their doing so however there is no doubt that the entire Russian Revolutionary intellectual tradition, encompassing Vera Zasulich, Danielson and others, who had underscored the infirmities of Russian capitalism and whom Lenin had attacked for their Narodnik views, also played a role. Notwithstanding their very different perspective from the Bolsheviks, they left an imprint on Bolshevik thinking on the specificity of the new situation.

But while this particular conceptual break involving the role of the peasantry occurred at an earlier date (there was to be a further revision in the Bolshevik position on the agrarian question at the time of the revolution, when the distribution of landownership among peasants replaced the earlier Bolshevik demand for the "nationalisation of land"), the conceptual break involving imperialism followed the outbreak of the First World War. In the entire debate between Lenin and the Narodniks on the possibility of a direct transition from the mir to socialism, and between Lenin and several Menshevik writers on whether to ally with the bourgeoisie or the peasantry in the democratic revolution, the focus had always been on a revolution in Russia in isolation. There had hardly ever been any reference to imperialism.

With the First World War however, this changed and imperialism came to the forefront of discussion. If imperialism had knit the world, and no major issue of the time could be discussed, as Lenin later put it, without reference to imperialism, then the fate of the Russian Revolution too was linked to imperialism. But here it became clear that the very phenomenon of inter-imperialist rivalry that caused wars and hence brought revolutions on the agenda, also made possible the survival of revolutions where they occurred. This rivalry actually provided the space for revolutions to survive.

The world in short had entered an era of revolutions. The imperialist chain was breaking, starting with its weakest link. The point was clearly to press ahead with the agenda of revolution, "going it alone" where necessary without waiting for the various "vacillating" elements in the working class leadership to join the revolutionary struggle.

Even in one of his last writings, Lenin emphasised that the Russian Revolution had survived because of inter-imperialist rivalry. And even after the failure of the German Revolution he was hopeful that China and India would witness revolutions, and added that Russia, China and India together constituted a large chunk of humanity. Revolutions in other words could no longer be considered in isolation; they were all interlinked. They were simply the moments of a world revolutionary transformation, confined not just to the advanced capitalist countries but covering the oppressed third world countries as well. Accordingly the Third International that was set up following the Bolshevik Revolution was something the like of which the world had never seen: at its Congresses, delegates from Germany, France and Britain rubbed shoulders with those from China, Indonesia, India and Vietnam. It was an International in the true sense of the term.

The Soviet Union has collapsed; the conjuncture of inter-imperialist rivalry that had characterised Lenin's period and indeed the entire period till the end of the Second World War, has given way to a new world situation characterised by the hegemony of international finance capital. The precise manner in which revolutions will occur in this new situation may not be identical with the way they had occurred earlier; this is something which will have to be worked out afresh. But the basic perspective on world revolution that had informed the October Revolution, namely of a set of interlinked revolutions, some sustained by the "working people" (where the worker-peasant alliance is the need of the hour), and others by the "working class" (where the peasantry is no longer a significant force), remains valid to this day. Indeed, the theory of revolution underlying the October Revolution which is built around the phenomenon of imperialism and the fact that it has knit the world will remain valid as long as imperialism exists.

(*People's Democracy,* November 6, 2016)

3

Draft Theses on National and Colonial Question

V. I. Lenin

1. An abstract or formal posing of the problem of equality in general and national equality in particular is in the very nature of bourgeois democracy. Under the guise of the equality of the individual in general, bourgeois democracy proclaims the formal or legal equality of the property-owner and the proletarian, the exploiter and the exploited, thereby grossly deceiving the oppressed classes. On the plea that all men are absolutely equal, the bourgeoisie is transforming the idea of equality, which is itself a reflection of relations in commodity production, into a weapon in its struggle against the abolition of classes. The real meaning of the demand for equality consists in its being a demand for the abolition of classes.
2. In conformity with its fundamental task of combating bourgeois democracy and exposing its falseness and hypocrisy, the Communist Party, as the avowed champion of the proletarian struggle to overthrow the bourgeois yoke, must base its policy, in the national question too, not on abstract and formal

principles but, first, on a precise appraisal of the specific historical situation and, primarily, of economic conditions; second, on a clear distinction between the interests of the oppressed classes, of working and exploited people, and the general concept of national interests as a whole, which implies the interests of the ruling class; third, on an equally clear distinction between the oppressed, dependent and subject nations and the oppressing, exploiting and sovereign nations, in order to counter the bourgeois-democratic lies that play down this colonial and financial enslavement of the vast majority of the world's population by an insignificant minority of the richest and advanced capitalist countries, a feature characteristic of the era of finance capital and imperialism.

3. The imperialist war of 1914-18 has very clearly revealed to all nations and to the oppressed classes of the whole world the falseness of bourgeois-democratic phrases, by practically demonstrating that the Treaty of Versailles of the celebrated "Western democracies" is an even more brutal and foul act of violence against weak nations than was the Treaty of Brest-Litovsk of the German Junkers and the Kaiser. The League of Nations and the entire post war policy of the Entente reveal this truth with even greater clarity and distinctness. They are everywhere intensifying the revolutionary struggle both of the proletariat in the advanced countries and of the toiling masses in the colonial and dependent countries. They are hastening the collapse of the petty-bourgeois nationalist illusions that nations can live together in peace and equality under capitalism.

4. From these fundamental premises it follows that the Communist International's entire policy on the national and the colonial questions should rest primarily on a closer union of the proletarians and the working masses of all nations and countries for a joint revolutionary struggle to overthrow the landowners and the bourgeoisie. This union alone will guarantee victory over

capitalism, without which the abolition of national oppression and inequality is impossible.

5. The world political situation has now placed the dictatorship of the proletariat on the order of the day. World political developments are of necessity concentrated on a single focus – the struggle of the world bourgeoisie against the Soviet Russian Republic, around which are inevitably grouped, on the one hand, the Soviet movements of the advanced workers in all countries, and, on the other, all the national liberation movements in the colonies and among the oppressed nationalities, who are learning from bitter experience that their only salvation lies in the Soviet system's victory over world imperialism.
6. Consequently, one cannot at present confine oneself to a bare recognition or proclamation of the need for closer union between the working people of the various nations; a policy must be pursued that will achieve the closest alliance, with Soviet Russia, of all the national and colonial liberation movements. The form of this alliance should be determined by the degree of development of the communist movement in the proletariat of each country, or of the bourgeois-democratic liberation movement of the workers and peasants in backward countries or among backward nationalities.
7. Federation is a transitional form to the complete unity of the working people of different nations. The feasibility of federation has already been demonstrated in practice both by the relations between the R.S.F.S.R. and other Soviet Republics (the Hungarian, Finnish, and Latvian in the past, and the Azerbaijan and Ukrainian at present), and by the relations within the R.S.F.S.R. in respect of nationalities which formerly enjoyed neither statehood nor autonomy (e.g., the Bashkir and Tatar autonomous republics in the R.S.F.S.R., founded in 1919 and 1920 respectively).
8. In this respect, it is the task of the Communist International to further develop and also to study and test by experience these

new federations, which are arising on the basis of the Soviet system and the Soviet movement. In recognising that federation is a transitional form to complete unity, it is necessary to strive for ever closer federal unity, bearing in mind, first, that the Soviet republics, surrounded as they are by the imperialist powers of the whole world – which from the military standpoint are immeasurably stronger – cannot possibly continue to exist without the closest alliance; second, that a close economic alliance between the Soviet republics is necessary, otherwise the productive forces which have been ruined by imperialism cannot be restored and the well-being of the working people cannot be ensured; third, that there is a tendency towards the creation of a single world economy, regulated by the proletariat of all nations as an integral whole and according to a common plan. This tendency has already revealed itself quite clearly under capitalism and is bound to be further developed and consummated under socialism.

9. The Communist International's national policy in the sphere of relations within the state cannot be restricted to the bare, formal, purely declaratory and actually non-committal recognition of the equality of nations to which the bourgeois democrats confine themselves – both those who frankly admit being such, and those who assume the name of socialists (such as the socialists of the Second International).

In all their propaganda and agitation – both within parliament and outside it – the Communist parties must consistently expose that constant violation of the equality of nations and of the guaranteed rights of national minorities which is to be seen in all capitalist countries, despite their "democratic" constitutions. It is also necessary, first, constantly to explain that only the Soviet system is capable of ensuring genuine equality of nations, by uniting first the proletarians and then the whole mass of the working population in the struggle against the bourgeoisie; and, second, that all Communist parties should render direct aid to the revolutionary movements among the dependent and underprivileged nations (for example, Ireland, the American Negroes, etc.) and in the colonies.

Without the latter condition, which is particularly important, the struggle against the oppression of dependent nations and colonies, as well as recognition of their right to secede, are but a false signboard, as is evidenced by the parties of the Second International.

10. Recognition of internationalism in word, and its replacement in deed by petty-bourgeois nationalism and pacifism, in all propaganda, agitation and practical work, is very common, not only among the parties of the Second International, but also among those which have withdrawn from it, and often even among parties which now call themselves communist. The urgency of the struggle against this evil, against the most deep-rooted petty-bourgeois national prejudices, looms ever larger with the mounting exigency of the task of converting the dictatorship of the proletariat from a national dictatorship (i.e., existing in a single country and incapable of determining world politics) into an international one (i.e., a dictatorship of the proletariat involving at least several advanced countries, and capable of exercising a decisive influence upon world politics as a whole). Petty-bourgeois nationalism proclaims as internationalism the mere recognition of the equality of nations, and nothing more. Quite apart from the fact that this recognition is purely verbal, petty-bourgeois nationalism preserves national self-interest intact, whereas proletarian internationalism demands, first, that the interests of the proletarian struggle in any one country should be subordinated to the interests of that struggle on a world-wide scale, and, second, that a nation which is achieving victory over the bourgeoisie should be able and willing to make the greatest national sacrifices for the overthrow of international capital.

Thus, in countries that are already fully capitalist and have workers' parties that really act as the vanguard of the proletariat, the struggle against opportunist and petty-bourgeois pacifist distortions of the concept and policy of internationalism is a primary and cardinal task.

11. With regard to the more backward states and nations, in which feudal or patriarchal and patriarchal-peasant relations predominate, it is particularly important to bear in mind:

    First, that all Communist parties must assist the bourgeois-democratic liberation movement in these countries, and that the duty of rendering the most active assistance rests primarily with the workers of the country the backward nation is colonially or financially dependent on;

    Second, the need for a struggle against the clergy and other influential reactionary and medieval elements in backward countries;

    Third, the need to combat Pan-Islamism and similar trends, which strive to combine the liberation movement against European and American imperialism with an attempt to strengthen the positions of the khans, landowners, mullahs, etc.;

    Fourth, the need, in backward countries, to give special support to the peasant movement against the landowners, against landed proprietorship, and against all manifestations or survivals of feudalism, and to strive to lend the peasant movement the most revolutionary character by establishing the closest possible alliance between the West European communist proletariat and the revolutionary peasant movement in the East, in the colonies, and in the backward countries generally. It is particularly necessary to exert every effort to apply the basic principles of the Soviet system in countries where pre-capitalist relations predominate – by setting up "working people's Soviets", etc.;

Fifth, the need for a determined struggle against attempts to give a communist colouring to bourgeois-democratic liberation trends in the backward countries; the Communist International should support bourgeois-democratic national movements in colonial and backward countries only on condition that, in these countries, the elements of future proletarian parties, which will be communist not only in name, are brought together and trained to understand their special tasks, i.e., those of the struggle against the bourgeois-democratic movements within their own nations. The Communist International must enter into a temporary alliance with bourgeois democracy in the colonial and backward countries, but should not merge with it, and should under all circumstances uphold the independence of the proletarian movement even if it is in its most embryonic form;

Sixth, the need constantly to explain and expose among the broadest working masses of all countries, and particularly of the backward countries, the deception systematically practised by the imperialist powers, which, under the guise of politically independent states, set up states that are wholly dependent upon them economically, financially and militarily. Under present-day international conditions there is no salvation for dependent and weak nations except in a union of Soviet republics.

12. The age-old oppression of colonial and weak nationalities by the imperialist powers has not only filled the working masses of the oppressed countries with animosity towards the oppressor nations, but has also aroused distrust in these nations in general, even in their proletariat. The despicable betrayal of socialism by the majority of the official leaders of this proletariat in 1914-19, when "defence of country" was used as a social-chauvinist cloak to conceal the defence of the "right" of their "own" bourgeoisie to oppress colonies and fleece financially dependent countries, was certain to enhance this perfectly legitimate distrust. On the

other hand, the more backward the country, the stronger is the hold of small-scale agricultural production, patriarchalism and isolation, which inevitably lend particular strength and tenacity to the deepest of petty-bourgeois prejudices, i.e., to national egoism and national narrow-mindedness. These prejudices are bound to die out very slowly, for they can disappear only after imperialism and capitalism have disappeared in the advanced countries, and after the entire foundation of the backward countries' economic life has radically changed. It is therefore the duty of the class-conscious communist proletariat of all countries to regard with particular caution and attention the survivals of national sentiments in the countries and among nationalities which have been oppressed the longest; it is equally necessary to make certain concessions with a view to more rapidly overcoming this distrust and these prejudices. Complete victory over capitalism cannot be won unless the proletariat and, following it, the mass of working people in all countries and nations throughout the world voluntarily strive for alliance and unity.

(V.I. Lenin, *Collected Works*, Volume 31, 2nd English Edition, Progress Publishers, Moscow, 1965)

4

Supplementary Theses on the National and Colonial Question

M.N. Roy

1. One of the most important questions that faces the Second Congress of the Communist International is to establish exactly the mutual relations between the Communist International and the revolutionary movement in politically oppressed countries dominated by their own capitalist system, like India and China. The history of the world revolution is living through a period which requires a correct conception of this mutual relationship. The Great European war and its consequences have shown clearly that the masses of people in the oppressed non-European countries have, as a result of the centralisation of world capitalism, been indissolubly bound up with the proletarian movement in Europe, which found an expression during the war, for example, in the sending of colonial troops and numerous masses of workers to the front.
2. European capitalism draws its strength in the main not so much from the industrial countries of Europe as from its colonial possessions. Its existence depends on control of extensive colonial

markets and a broad field of opportunities for exploitation. England, the bulwark of imperialism, has already suffered from overproduction for a century. Without the extensive colonial possessions that are essential for the sale of her goods and at the same time form the source of her raw materials, the capitalist order in England would long since have collapsed under its own weight. At the same time that British imperialism makes hundreds of millions of the inhabitants of Asia and Africa into slaves, it also keeps the British proletariat under the domination of the bourgeoisie.

3. The super-profits made in the colonies form one of the main sources of the resources of contemporary capitalism. The European working class will only succeed in overthrowing the capitalist order once this source has finally been stopped up. The capitalist countries try, not indeed without success, to restore their shaky position by extensive and intensive exploitation of human labour and the natural wealth of the colonies. As a result of the exploitation of the colonial population European imperialism is in a position to grant the labour aristocracy in Europe a whole range of concessions. While on the one hand European imperialism tries to force down the absolute minimum level necessary to keep the proletariat alive by the import of goods produced by the cheaper labour power of the workers of the colonial countries, it is on the other hand prepared to sacrifice the increased profits it could make in the home country in order to receive the super-profits it can obtain by exploitation in the colonies.

4. The loss of the colonies and the proletarian revolution in the mother countries will bring the downfall of the capitalist order in Europe. In consequence the Communist International must extend its field of activity. The Communist International must enter into much closer connection with the revolutionary forces that are at present participating in the overthrow of imperialism

in the politically and economically oppressed countries. The collaboration of these two forces is necessary for the complete success of the world revolution.

5. The Communist International is the concentrated will of the world proletariat. Its task is the organisation of the working class of the whole world for the overthrow of the capitalist order and for the spread of communism. The Communist International is a warlike unity that must unite the revolutionary forces of every country in the world. The Second International, permeated through and through with bourgeois culture and led by a handful of political dilettantes, underestimated the whole importance of the colonial question. The world outside simply did not exist as far as they were concerned. They did not recognise the necessity of the collaboration of the revolutionary movement in Europe and the other parts of the world. Instead of supporting the revolutionary movement in the colonies both materially and morally, the members of the Second International themselves became imperialists.

6. The foreign imperialism violently forced upon the peoples of the East has without doubt hindered their social and economic development and robbed them of the opportunity of reaching the same level of development as has been achieved in Europe and America. Thanks to the imperialist policies whose efforts are directed towards holding up industrial development in the colonies, the native proletariat has only come into existence fairly recently. The dispersed local cottage industries have given way to the centralised industries of the imperialist countries. As a result the vast majority of the population was forced to engage in agriculture and export raw materials abroad. On the other hand we can observe a rapidly growing concentration of the land in the hands of big landowners, capitalists and the state, which again contributes to the growth of the number of landless peasants. The vast majority of the population of these colonies

lives under conditions of oppression. As a result of these policies the underdeveloped spirit of outrage that lives in the masses of the people can only find an expression in the numerically small intellectual middle class. Foreign domination constantly obstructs the free development of social life; therefore the revolution's first step must be the removal of this foreign domination. The struggle to overthrow foreign domination in the colonies does not therefore mean underwriting the national aims of the national bourgeoisie but much rather smoothing the path to liberation for the proletariat of the colonies.

7. Two movements can be discerned which are growing further and further apart with every day that passes. One of them is the bourgeois-democratic nationalist movement, which pursues the programme of political liberation with the conservation of the capitalist order; the other is the struggle of the propertyless peasants for their liberation from every kind of exploitation. The first movement attempts, often with success, to control the second; the Communist International must however, fight against any such control, and the development of the class consciousness of the working masses of the colonies must consequently be directed towards the overthrow of foreign capitalism. The most important and necessary task however, is the creation of Communist organisations of peasants and workers in order to lead them to the revolution and the setting up of the Soviet Republic. In this way the masses of the people in the backward countries will be brought to communism not by capitalist development but by the development of class consciousness under the leadership of the proletariat of the advanced countries.

8. The real strength, the foundation of the liberation movement, will not allow itself to be forced into the narrow framework of bourgeois-democratic nationalism in the colonies. In the greater part of the colonies there already exist organised revolutionary parties which work in close contact with the working masses.

The Communist International must make contact with the revolutionary movements in the colonies through the mediation of these parties and groups, for they are the vanguard of the working class. At present they are not numerous, but they express the will of the working class and lead the revolution behind them. The Communist Parties of the various imperialist countries must work in the closest contact with the proletarian parties of the proletarian countries and through them support the revolutionary movement in general both materially and morally.

9. In the first period the revolution in the colonies will not be communist; if however from the very start the communist vanguard emerges at its head the revolutionary masses will be brought on to the correct path along which, through the gradual gathering of revolutionary experience, they will reach the hidden goal. It would be a mistake to try to solve the agrarian question straight away according to purely communist principles. In the first stage of its development the revolution in the colonies must be carried out according to the programme of purely petty-bourgeois demands, such as distribution of the land and so on. But from this it must not be concluded that the leadership in the colonies can be allowed to fall into the hands of the bourgeois democrats. On the contrary, the proletarian parties must carry out an intensive propaganda of communist ideas and found workers' and peasants' councils at the first opportunity. These councils must work in the same way as the Soviet Republics in the advanced capitalist countries in order to bring about the final overthrow of the capitalist order throughout the whole world.

(*Minutes of the Proceedings*, Volume One and Two, Second Congress of the Communist International)

Aurora: Russian Cruiser which gave signal of revolution (1917)

HMIS Hindustan: Ship of Royal Indian Navy occupied by revolutionary naval ratings (1946)

Part 2

Pre-Independence Period

Sohan Singh Bhakna (second from right) and other Ghadarites, 1915.

Women's march in Bombay during Quit India Movement, 1942.

Introduction (Part 2)

The pre-independence phase of the relationship between the Russian Revolution and the Indian Freedom Struggle has a long history. The earliest connection probably goes back to the formation of the Ghadar Party, a group of Indian emigrants in Canada and USA who were politicised by the racism they faced in these countries. The Ghadar Party was secular and wanted a federal republican government of free India. Its activities led to a tightening of immigration laws in North America. Many members of the Ghadar Party left Canada and the USA to come to India and revolt against the British. They plotted a mutiny in the British Indian Army against the Raj, were tried and convicted by the British in the first Lahore Conspiracy Case in 1915, a precursor to the many conspiracy cases that revolutionaries would be involved in. A total of 291 conspirators were put on trial. Of these 42 were awarded the death sentence, 114 transported for life, and 93 awarded varying terms of imprisonment. The evidence of their resolve is in a remark made by one of them on being handed the death sentence, "Is that all? Can't you award something more?" It is to be remembered that the period of 1914-1918 was that of the First World War.

Many Indians were affected by the Russian Revolution in 1917. A prominent figure among them was M.N. Roy who helped found the Communist Party of Mexico in 1919. Roy attended the Second Congress of the Communist International in 1920 and subsequently formed an Indian Communist Party in Tashkent in 1920 which influenced many *Muhajirs* who reached Tashkent via Afghanistan. *Muhajir* refers to Indian youth who were part of the *Khilafat* movement (a movement of Indian Muslims against British imperialism). Several young (and old) students from both the Ghadar Party and the *Muhajirs* would go to the University of Toilers of the East, in Moscow, and become firm communists. Hence, M.N. Roy and others abroad were influential in propagating communism in India, and exchanged correspondence with many local leaders in India.

Meanwhile, in India, Gandhiji launched the non-cooperation movement in 1920, and joined with the Khilafat movement. Communist groups emerged in India in 1921 under leaders like Muzaffar Ahmad, S.A. Dange and Ghulam Hussein. These were in industrial centers with trade union movements. The first Indian communist conference was convened at Kanpur from December 25-28, 1925 which led to the formation of the Communist Party of India. The communist leaders had called for complete independence from the British at a very early stage, and were consequently charged in several conspiracy cases for plotting to overthrow the British Raj. The Kanpur Conspiracy Case in 1924 played an important role in spreading the communist ideology in India. The communist leader from Bombay, Sripad Amrit Dange, wrote a booklet 'Gandhi vs Lenin' which was taken as evidence that the communists were trying to conspire against the King Emperor. The media coverage of the trial helped spread the ideology of communism among ordinary people. In 1929, the Britishers were afraid that the Comintern was trying to stoke a revolution in India. They therefore targeted trade unionists, labour leaders and communists in the Meerut Conspiracy Case. The trials were highly publicised and demonstrated the growing radicalisation of the Indian youth.

This period is also significant for the formation of the Hindustan Socialist Republic Association in 1928, the Salt March and the Chittagong armed uprising, both in 1930. Finally, the Second World War in 1938 sparked another set of revolutionary activities. The Quit India Movement was launched in 1942. It was in the February of 1946 that the Royal Indian Navy mutinied and it was followed by the call of the Communist Party for a general strike. These and many other incidents simultaneously culminated into India's independence in 1947. The articles selected cover this period and many of the events mentioned above. The article by C. Rajeswara Rao mentions the importance of the geographical location of Russia being partly in Asia, and the importance of Lenin's concept of the unity of Russia, India and China. The article by Gangadhar Adhikari takes a broad view of the link between the October Revolution and the Indian National Movement, dividing it into three parts and going through much of the history mentioned above. The article by C. Achutha Menon gives some background into the significance of the October Revolution for the leaders of the main thrust of the anti-colonial movement led by the Congress Party, including Jawaharlal Nehru, Gandhi and Subhash Chandra Bose. The article by Bijoy Kumar Sinha is very interesting, and goes through the influence of the Russian Revolution, the Ghadar Party and the Comintern on the thinking and practice of Bhagat Singh and others in the Hindustan Socialist Republic Association. Finally, the article by Hajrah Begum discusses the impact of the October Revolution on Indian women. It takes up the role of Indian women as trade unionists and active participants in political struggle. It also mentions that the Soviet Union served as a model in its ability to further women's rights much more than 'advanced' capitalist countries.

Meerut Conspiracy Case, 1929

The British government was increasingly worried about the growing influence of the communists in India. They feared that the Comintern was trying to stoke a revolution in India by sending some British communists. Hence the government targeted labour leaders, trade unionists, Communist Party members and British communists. In March 1929, thirty two people were arrested from various parts of India. These people were charged of conspiracy to deprive the King of the sovereignty of British India. There were three British citizens among the accused — Philip Spratt, Benjamin Francis Bradley and Lester Hutchinson. The court pronounced sentences in January 1933. Twenty-seven accused were given transportation of varying durations. Prima facie this led to the weakening of the organisation of communist movement. But the trials made these people heroes and the accused used the courtroom to propagate their ideas. The newspapers and journals carried the speeches made in the courtroom and the nation was infused with communist ideas. The trial also demonstrated the growing radicalisation of Indian youth against the British government.

Portrait of 25 of the Meerut prisoners taken outside the jail. Back row (left to right): K.N. Sehgal, S.S. Josh, H.L. Hutchinson, Shaukat Usmani, B.F. Bradley, A. Prasad, P. Spratt, G. Adhikari. Middle Row: R.R. Mitra, Gopen Chakravarti, Kishori Lal Ghosh, L.R. Kadam, D.R. Thengdi, Goura Shanker, S. Bannerjee, K.N. Joglekar, P.C. Joshi, Muzaffar Ahmad. Front Row: M.G. Desai, D. Goswami, R.S. Nimbkar, S.S. Mirajkar, S.A. Dange, S.V. Ghate, Gopal Basak.

5

October Socialist Revolution and Impact on India and Asia

C. Rajeswara Rao

This year we are celebrating the 70th anniversary of the Great October Revolution which had opened a new golden era in the history of mankind. For the first time political power had passed into the hands of the toiling people, headed by the working class.

All exploitation and oppression was ended. A fraternal union of the various nationalities emerged in place of the oppressive czarist Empire. Since then the Soviet Union has become the harbinger and inspiration of the toiling people throughout the world.

The immortal Lenin who led the revolution lost no time in spreading its message to the peoples of the world. He organised the Communist International and gathered the communist revolutionaries under its banner.

He enriched the historic slogan given by the founders of communism Karl Marx and Friedrich Engels, "workers of the world unite", by changing it to "workers of the world and oppressed peoples unite". Thereby he declared that the people of the countries groaning under the yoke of imperialism are the allies of the proletariat of the imperialist countries. Hence he urged upon the proletariat to support the struggle of the oppressed peoples without any reservations.

He consistently fought against the right-wing social democrats who played the role of 'apologists of imperialist oppression' in one way or the other. Lenin also gave a direction to the communist revolutionaries of the countries oppressed by imperialism through his famous thesis "National and Colonial Question", adopted by the second congress of the Communist International held in 1920.

He urged upon the communist parties of advanced capitalist countries to give all political and practical help to the freedom movements and the communists of these oppressed countries. He enjoined upon the communists of these countries to support the freedom movements led by the bourgeoisie while maintaining their independent identity.

It is a matter of great importance that the Soviet Union belongs to both the continents of Europe and Asia. Because of this geographical factor the Great October Socialist Revolution and the Soviet Union had greatly influenced the development of the freedom and communist movements in the continent of Asia. The phenomenal development of the Asiatic nationalities of the Soviet Union from backward states into advanced socialist nationalities has greatly influenced the Asiatic countries.

The Great October Socialist Revolution and the Soviet Union had made a great impact on India also. Lenin paid special attention to India and China because of their vast size and importance. While dealing with the outcome of the proletarian struggle on a world scale, he said, "in the final analysis the outcome of the struggle will be determined by the fact that Russia, India and China, etc. account for the overwhelming majority of the population of the globe". Lenin met many Indian revolutionaries like Raja Mahendra Pratap Singh, Maulana Barkatullah, M.N. Roy and Virendra Chattopadhyay who were in Europe at that time and helped them to understand the then world situation and their task in rallying the Indian masses for the liberation of India from British imperialism.

India's Struggle

The Great October Socialist Revolution and the Soviet Union had also influenced a number of leaders of our country's freedom struggle. Even Mahatma Gandhi, who had opposed the theory of class struggle and advocated non-violence, said:

> It is my firm conviction that nothing enduring can be built on violence. But, be that as it may, there is no questioning the fact that the Bolshevik ideal has behind it the purest sacrifice of countless men and women, who have given up their all for its sake; an ideal that is sanctified by sacrifices of such master spirits as Lenin cannot go in vain. (*Young India*, November 5, 1928)

The late Prime Minister and renowned world statesman Jawaharlal Nehru had repeatedly emphasised the example of the Soviet Union in solving the problems of poverty, unemployment and other ills of capitalism. In his famous book *Discovery of India* (1945) he said:

> I have no doubt that the Soviet revolution had advanced society by a great leap and had lit a bright flame that could not be smothered, and that it had laid the foundation for that new civilisation towards which the world could advance.

Mahatma Gandhi rallied the urge of the people for freedom after the First World War and led a countrywide struggle of non-cooperation against British imperialism. However, the struggle was abruptly discontinued since the people in their anger indulged in violence which led to great demoralisation.

It is after this that the various communist groups in India who were working separately came together to form the Communist Party of India in 1925. It attracted to its fold not only a number of left congressmen but also many national revolutionaries of the famous Ghadar Party, of Bhagat Singh's Naujawan Bharat Sabha and of other "terrorist" groups.

At the behest of the Communist International the Communist Party of Great Britain sent some communist leaders to help the young Communist Party for the organisation of the working class and other mass organisations.

It is to the credit to the Communist Party of India that it was the first to raise the issue of complete independence on the forum of the Congress, and outside, through its representatives. It organised the working class in Bombay, Calcutta, Madras and some other cities and led their heroic strikes. It also organised the peasants against feudal oppression. It organised students, women and other sections of the people, but also infused anti-imperialist consciousness into them and brought them into the freedom struggle.

British Animosity

The British imperialists had never taken kindly towards the communist movement in India. They wanted to nip it in the bud. They arrested and jailed communist leaders in 1924 and 1928 under various conspiracy cases. Consequently, the Communist Party was forced to work underground for most of the time during the domination of British imperialism.

The end of the Second World War brought a new stage in our country's freedom struggle. The historic victory over fascism, the super-human sacrifices made by the Soviet people in the Great Patriotic War against Hitler's armies, the emergence of the socialist community and the weakening of imperialism had enthused the oppressed peoples throughout the world. The colonial system broke up under the hammer blows of freedom movements in various parts of the world. Many countries gained political independence.

In India, a revolutionary post-war upsurge broke out against British imperialism in the form of demonstrations against the trials of Indian National Army leaders. The British imperialists tried to suppress these struggles with a heavy hand.

In this connection the historic rebellion of the Indian naval ratings took place followed by revolts in the Indian Air Force and Army units. The Bombay working class under the leadership of the Communist Party of India supported the naval revolt with a general

Second World War and the Royal Indian Navy Mutiny

The Second World War initially started as an intra-imperialist war between German Fascism and British imperialism. However, Hitler planned to first conquer and attack the Soviet Union and use their resources to eventually defeat the British. It was the heroic effort of the Soviet Union, in particular the battle of Stalingrad, that played the decisive role in stopping the advance of German Fascism and defeating it. Meanwhile, over two million Indian soldiers fought on the side of the British Army against Hitler. As a result there was significant resentment in the army against the British. It is worth mentioning that Subhash Chandra Bose's Indian National Army, even though a military failure had the symbolic effect of imagining an army that belonged to a free India. This was the background that led to the mutiny of the Royal Indian Navy. What started as a strike by about a 1000 ratings became a mutiny of the entire Indian Navy. Aruna Asaf Ali was one of the leaders of the Congress who supported the mutiny. The Communist Party of India gave a call for a general strike which received a huge response. However, the Congress leadership unfortunately decided not to support the strike and asked the ratings to pull back. The Royal Indian Navy Mutiny is also significant because at a time of communal tension, and disagreement between the Muslim League and the Congress, the ratings raised slogans of "Hindu-Muslim Ek Ho" and "Down with Imperialism".

EN-VOGUE

Evening News

OF INDIA

DHANKI

MINERVA

R.I.N. Ratings In Open Mutiny

strike in which hundreds of workers were shot down. After that the All India Railway and Postal Workers called for countrywide general strikes. In the same period the peasants in rural areas also started struggles against landlord oppression. The British imperialists saw the writing on the wall and quit the country after partitioning it into the Indian Union and Pakistan.

The CPI played a significant role in the post-war upsurge against British imperialism and the abolition of princely states and unification of the country. The great struggles of Telangana and Punnapra-Vayalar against recalcitrant princes who refused to join the Indian Union were led by the CPI with arms in hand. Thus the CPI made great sacrifices in the freedom struggle led by the Congress and enriched it in its own way.

The attainment of freedom by a big country like India was an important event. During the last 40 years of independence, India had to foil many conspiracies of imperialists with the help of the Soviet Union and other socialist countries to preserve and strengthen its own freedom. Indian people do realise that Soviet Union stands by them at all critical times in the post-war period. Not only this, the Soviet Union and other friendly socialist countries have helped India to develop its basic industries like steel, oil, heavy machine building, coal and power, all of which have made India self-reliant to the chagrin of the imperialists.

Indo-Soviet Cooperation

All this was possible because of the close Indo-Soviet cooperation in the economic, technological and political fields. The 70 giant industrial complexes that were built with the help of the Soviet Union in various parts of our country stand as living symbols of Indo-Soviet friendship.

CPI is proud that it had played a significant role in the strengthening of Indo-Soviet friendship and cooperation carried out by the late Prime Ministers Jawaharlal Nehru, Indira Gandhi as well as the present Prime Minister Rajiv Gandhi.

We are also proud that our country has been playing an important role in the preservation of world peace, supporting the anti-imperialist struggles of the peoples of other countries through its progressive foreign policy since independence. CPI has been ever vigilant against internal and external reaction which wanted to sabotage the progressive foreign policy of our country and had been playing an important role in foiling these conspiracies.

Now it has fallen to the lot of the land of Lenin, the Soviet Union, for heading the struggle for world peace, to save humanity from a nuclear disaster. Science has developed to such an extent in various fields that it can be misused for destroying human civilisation itself or it can be used for further happiness of humanity. It was the Soviet Union, other countries of the socialist community and the world communist movement that had raised the question of the need for preventing a Third World War which is bound to be a nuclear war.

They also envisaged the possibility of preventing such a possibility if all the world peace forces were united, irrespective of political opinions. The repeated initiatives that the Soviet Union has taken for the prevention of nuclear arms race and elimination of nuclear weapons altogether by the year 2000 have received the support of peace-loving humanity throughout the world.

The latest proposal of the CPSU General Secretary, Mikhail Gorbachev for the elimination of medium and short range nuclear missiles of the Soviet Union and USA in Europe has been agreed to in principle by the US president Ronald Reagan. This is a good augury for further progress towards elimination of the nuclear threat.

This was possible because of strengthening world public opinion, especially in the western capitalist countries, in favour of Gorbachev's proposals. There cannot be any complacency in the matter. The peace movement must be taken to newer sections of the people especially under the influence of the conservative parties in Europe.

In this connection, I must say that the phenomenal changes that are taking place in the Soviet Union, i.e. 'Perestroika' (restructuring), 'glasnost' (openness)[1] and strengthening of democracy are also influencing world public opinion in favour of the Soviet Union. This is making socialism more attractive to the common people throughout the world. Anti-Soviet and anti-communist reactions propagated by imperialism are getting weakened.

In the end I must say that the latest article of Mikhail Gorbachev – "Reality and Guarantees for a secure world" – written on the occasion of the 42nd session of the UN General Assembly, is of immense importance.

The ideas and practical proposals that are presented in this article, not only for preventing a world war but also for using science, technology and the natural resources of the world for the good of humanity, would receive support of the widest sections of the people.

Objective Processes

The idea that "objective processes are making our complex and diverse world more and more inter-related and interdependent" and that "it increasingly needs a mechanism capable of discussing common problems in a responsible fashion" is unexceptionable. He stated that such a role can be played by the UN.

He has proposed that nuclear disarmament can release enough funds for solving the problems of the economy of developed countries, and that a part of this huge expenditure, if used for the

1 **Glasnost and Perestroika:** Talking about the unceasing efforts of the Soviet Union to strengthen the peace movement, Com. Rajeswara Rao has appreciated the nuclear disarmament proposal put forward by CPSU General Secretary Mikhail Gorbachev. He has also appreciated the programmes of Glasnost and Perestroika introduced by Gorbachev in 1986-87 as measures which would advance the democratic space in Soviet Union. In the late 1980s, the western media as well as the Soviet and East European intellectuals vociferously supported the two measures. When we analyse the introduction and implementation of Glasnost and Perestroika from hindsight, we reach the conclusion that these measures led to complete dismantling of the USSR. But in 1987, it was difficult to gauge the full implications of these moves which were being commended world over.

advancement of the developing countries, can mitigate the hunger of unfortunate people of these countries.

By this, Gorbachev does not mean a status quo which will enable the imperialists to maintain their rule forever in the capitalist countries and their continued economic domination over the developing countries. He stated in the clearest terms that "the right of the peoples to sovereignly choose the roads and forms of their development, revolutionary or evolutionary, is an imperative condition for universal security". He rules out any external interference from any quarter and destabilisation of existing governments from outside.

These important ideas for the security of humanity and social progress deserve the support of all well-meaning people of diverse political opinions. These ideas presented at the time of the historic 70th anniversary of the Great October Socialist Revolution are of immense world significance.

(*New Age Weekly*, November 08, 1987)

Women Soldiers of Telangana Armed Rebellion, 1946-51

Women played an important role in Telangana struggle. They suffered, starved under the regime of extortions of the Nizam and the Deshmukhs. With Telangana struggle, they now saw the possibility of a new life. They actually participated in the land movement in the seizure of grain and in the struggle for higher agricultural wages. They fought the Razakars and Nizam's Police and later the Indian Army standing shoulder to shoulder with their menfolk.

6

Great October and India's National Movement

G. Adhikari

Indian people join the progressive peoples and the working class of the whole world in felicitating the Soviet people, the Communist Party and its leaders on the 50th anniversary of the Great October Socialist Revolution. All of them, particularly we in India, are conscious that in celebrating the 50th birthday of the first socialist state, we are celebrating some of the revolutionary achievements of our own people who owed their inspiration to that great historic event.

The Red October of the Russians opened a new era in the history of all mankind. The guns of Aurora, which announced the seizure of power by the workers and peasants of Russia, simultaneously heralded the beginning of the world revolution. It was a revolution unprecedented in world history.

In all the former revolutions, one exploiting class had replaced another. In October Revolution, a new class had come to power – the modern working class – holding the levers of production of modern economy in its hands–a class which cannot liberate itself fully unless it goes on continually fighting for the liberation of all the other exploited classes and oppressed peoples.

We speak of the international significance of the October Revolution in the sense that it initiated the world revolutionary process of transition from capitalism to socialism. The problems it solved for Russia were simultaneously the problems connected with the basic contradictions both in the advanced capitalist countries of the West and in the vast oppressed countries of the East.

In advanced countries, the seething discontent of workers, struggling against the burdens of the imperialist war, and fighting for peace and the end of the war was rising. In the dependent countries of the East, an upsurge of National Liberation Movement was bursting forth.

It was against this background that the triumphant slogans of the October Revolution reverberated throughout the world. "end to the war", "peace without annexations and indemnities", "land to the peasants and end of landlordism", "taking over factories, mills, banks and mines", "overthrow of capitalism", "self-determination of nations by ensuring freedom of peoples enslaved by the Czarist Empire", "all power to the Soviets of workers, peasants and soldiers".

Triumphant Slogans Echoing Even Today

The bold and revolutionary implementation of these slogans by the workers and peasants of Russia electrified not only the working class of the countries of Europe but also the oppressed peoples of the dependent countries of the East.

The October Revolution hastened the end of war. Soon after began the revolutionary onslaught of the workers of Europe which toppled thrones and monarchies and shook the capitalist order in the West. In Asia began the unprecedented ferment and upsurge of the vast population of India, China and other countries that were fighting for freedom and independence from their foreign imperialist domination.

The impact of the October Revolution on the National Liberation Movement of India falls into three successive phases:

- In the first phase (1918-35), our independence movement entered the mass phase and with the rise of the organised working class movement and the Communist Party of India, it adopted a programme of complete independence with an anti-imperialist and anti-feudal content.
- In the second phase, it broadened out into a powerful, united and anti-imperialist democratic movement in which the organised working class and peasant movement emerged as independent political forces (see box). Freedom struggle reached its climax in the years of post-war upsurge. Our country won independence in the context of the second stage of general crisis of capitalism which was unleashed by the split and weakening of imperialist camp on one hand and the historic victory of USSR over Fascism on the other.
- The third phase is the present one, when politically independent India is saddled with tasks and difficulties of an unfinished

Anti-Imperialist United Front

As mentioned earlier, the Communist International had already decided in the Second Congress that they would support anti-imperialist national revolutionary movements. In the fourth congress, they put out the slogan of the anti-imperialist united front. The programme of this front included democratic political rights, agrarian reforms, progressive labour laws and the setting up of an independent republic in the colonies. It was emphasised that the peasants and working classes must maintain their independence from movements which were simply democratic, but must still support them in their struggles against imperialism. In India, it was the period during and after the Second World War that saw the crystallisation of this united front against British imperialism, which then led to independence. Here, it is worth mentioning the efforts of P.C. Joshi who was General Secretary of the Communist Party of India during that period and worked tirelessly to establish this united front, which attracted many intellectuals, artists, writers, etc. to the party.

democratic revolution. In the endeavour towards achieving economic independence and social progress, there is a sharp struggle. Will it lead to continued development of capitalism and growth of monopoly spelling untold suffering to the working people and danger to country's independence or will it move towards the completion of democratic revolution and advance to socialism?

Profound Influence in Each Phase

In each of these phases, the ideas and principles of the October Socialist Revolution – the achievements and actions which carried forward these ideas and principles into practice – had a profound influence on the developments in our country.

It was not at all surprising that the British imperialists with their die hard Churchill, who took the lead in launching the counter-revolutionary war of intervention against the young Soviet republic, should do their damndest worst to cordon off and blockade India from the influence of the socialist revolution, to unleash the foulest slander campaign against the same through their news agencies.

They framed draconic, repressive 'laws' to crush the revolutionary activities of the Nationalists, which increased in years of the First World War. They launched a campaign of terror and shootings to crush the mass protest movement against the same. As early as in 1919, they set up an 'anti-Bolshevik' department of their secret police to track down and destroy the rising new revolutionary and communist movement. These desperate efforts of the British imperialists did not stop the national liberation movement entering the new and mass phase, unleashed by the first Satyagraha and non-cooperation movement by Mahatma Gandhi, nor did they succeed in preventing the rise of the working class and communist movement.

The struggles and sacrifices of the various sections of the revolutionary wing of our national movement broke the imperialist bolstered blockade and made the ideas and achievements of the

Russian Revolution known to our people. Indian national revolutionaries active in Europe and America, democratic leaders of Indian National Movement, as well as progressive and patriotic publicists of our country, disregarded imperialist propaganda and recognised in this great event a turning point in world history. They saw that a new force had arisen. A force of revolutionary masses, challenging the warring imperialists – a force that was bound to be a friend of liberation struggles.

Thus we find that émigré revolutionaries of the First World War period like Virendranath Chattopadhyaya, Bhupendranath Dutta, Abanindranath Mukherji, M.N. Roy, Mahendra Pratap, Barkatullah, Khankhoje, Chempakaraman Pillay and M.P.T. Acharya and many others turned to revolutionary Russia and its leader Lenin for inspiration and support. A committee of National Revolutionaries in India addressed an appeal to Lenin asking for his support for India's fight for self-determination.

Pre-World War One stalwarts of our radical national movement like Lokamanya Bal Gangadhar Tilak, Lala Lajpat Rai and Bipin Chandra Pal went on record recognising the historic significance of the socialist revolution in Russia and rebuffing the slanderous propaganda against it by the British rulers in India. Mahatma Gandhi, though critical of the ideology of the Socialist Revolution, repudiated the bogey of 'Bolshevik menace' which the British were assiduously inculcating, and later expressed his goodwill toward Revolutionary Russia and admiration for its leader, Lenin.

Then we have the leaders and cadres of the Ghadar (Revolution) Party formed abroad by the Punjabi peasants who had migrated to California (USA) in search of labour. They attempted an armed uprising in India in the closing years of the First World War by sending a whole shipful of arms and fighting men. Most of them turned to the Soviet Union and Communism after the October Revolution. Among them are outstanding names such as Ratan Singh, Santokh Singh, Baba Sohan Singh Bhakna, Baba Gurmukh Singh and Teja Singh Swatantra.

Muhajarin Movement of Muslim Youth

Then we have the Muhajarin (migrant) movement of Muslim youth, inspired by nationalism in the course of the non-cooperation and Khilafat movement. They left India in hundreds in search of help for the independence struggle. Scores of them were attracted by the Russian Revolution and crossed over to the Soviet Union; many of them participated in the civil war in Central Asian parts of the Soviet Union and later went for political training.

When they secretly returned to India after scaling hazardous land routes with sore feet but stout hearts and nothing more dangerous with them than revolutionary pamphlets, they were arrested by the British police and sentenced to various terms of imprisonment in the Peshawar Communist Conspiracy cases. Among them are such names as Pheroze-ud-din Mansoor, Abdul Majid, Shaukat Usmani, Rafiq Ahmed and many others.

In India itself a large number of militant cadres participating in the mass upsurge of the first non-cooperation movement led by Mahatma Gandhi, but disconsolate with the limitations of his ideology and in search of new paths for India's independence, began to turn to the ideas of the October Revolution, to the theory and philosophy of scientific socialism. They applied these ideas in their struggles of India's freedom movement and in organising the masses of workers and peasants. It was out of these pioneering efforts that the early Communist groups were formed in Punjab, Maharashtra, Bengal and in Madras. S.A. Dange, Muzaffar Ahmad and Singaravelu Chettiar are some of the outstanding names of the early pioneers.

It was through the struggles and sacrifices of these various streams of the revolutionary wing of the national freedom movement, and the working class struggles of the early twenties that the Communist Party of India was formed. With the formation of Communist Party of India, militant class organisations of the industrial workers emerged and a new fighting programme and path for India's independence movement was formulated.

The emergence of this new force, which sought to give an ideological orientation and a revolutionary edge to the national movement, was not a conspiracy of a handful of 'Bolshevik agents' as the British imperialists hypocritically screamed to mislead the masses and to isolate the communists from the national stream. In their secret documents preparatory to launching the Kanpur and Meerut cases, the British imperialists frankly talked of discrediting and putting communist leaders out of action whose ideas were influencing certain left-wing leaders of the national movement.

These criminal designs of imperialism did not entirely succeed. Lenin's idea that Russia's socialist revolution has to ally itself with the awakening masses of the surrounding nations of the East was rooted in objective reality. As our national movement entered into its new phase and became consistently anti-imperialist, it naturally began to look to the socialist Soviet Union as its ally. Lenin paid the greatest attention to the contemporary national liberation movement and worked out the main guidelines of their development. He advised the emerging Communist Parties in these countries to fully support the national liberation movements inasmuch as they were revolutionary and to make them so. He wanted communists not to paint national movements in communist colours and, at the same time, to build independent working class organisation, strengthen the party and develop the peasant struggles against landlordism.

Lenin visualised that if these countries achieved independence in a revolutionary way, the revolutionary power that would emerge there would not be a proletarian dictatorship but a form of revolutionary democracy of peasants' Soviets, which with the assistance of the proletariat of the advanced socialist states would be able to make the transition to socialism without passing through the stage of development of capitalism.

Lenin's ideas, broadcast through the activities of the Communist International, largely influenced the communists and progressives in our country who were fighting to define the goal, the programme and path of our independence struggle.

The goal was complete independence from foreign imperialism. The programme was smashing the grip of British colonialists on our economy: abolishing landlordism and giving land to peasants: establishing democracy for the people. The path was the path of mass revolution, of awakening, mobilising and uniting the broad masses of the common people, the peasantry, the working class and the anti-imperialist national bourgeoisie.

This programme and perspective became the banner of the militant wing of our national movement. Its early beginnings were seen in the earlier writings of S.A. Dange (in Gandhi vs Lenin and the Socialist) and in manifestoes addressed by the CPI to the sessions of the national party congress in the early twenties. In a more mature form, it was put across from the prisoner's dock in the Meerut conspiracy case, which the communists converted into a platform for the indictment of British colonialists and for the propagation of their idea.

These ideas evolved and took more concrete shape in the fire of the great mass upsurge of national struggle unleashed by the second non-cooperation movement of the thirties, which was launched under the slogan of complete independence adopted by the Lahore session of the National Congress. They were consistently popularised by the organised working class movement which was moving forward as an independent political force.

The programme and perspective were being put forward not only by communists but by other revolutionary groups like that of the great patriot and martyr Bhagat Singh. They were popularised in a general way by Jawaharlal Nehru in his numerous speeches and writings of the thirties and later they found a very popular exposition in his presidential address to the Lucknow session of the National Congress (1936).

Socialism and Internationalism

Together with this, the progressive vanguard of our national movement was inspired by the ideals of Socialism that were being realised in the Soviet Union. It was also inspired by the idea of internationalism – that our independence struggle was an indivisible part of the world struggle for peace, freedom and socialism.

The bonds of friendship that were forged between the October Revolution and our national movement in its first phase are expressed in incidents, actions and in the creative works of literature. The memory of Murtaza Ali, who deserted from the invading British Army to the Soviet side and fought as a partisan in the ranks of the Red Army defending the revolution in the Central Asian parts of the Soviet Union is treasured in the USSR. As early as in 1921, the Jharia session of the All India Trade Union Congress expressed solidarity with Russian workers and people who were then affected by famine. In 1928 the Russian trade unions sent a generous assistance to the striking textile workers of Bombay who had built the first militant working class trade union in India.

Later on, expression of solidarity with the workers' and peasants' socialist state in the Soviet Union became a normal feature of the militant working class and peasant movement in India.

The visits of Motilal Nehru, Jawaharlal Nehru and Rabindranath Tagore to the Soviet Union, and the tributes paid to the achievements of socialism in the writings of the latter two have historic significance. Especially, the poet's "Letters from Russia" is a document of emotional commitment, which truly reflects how the Indian masses stirred by the freedom upsurge of the thirties looked to the socialist achievements of the Soviet Union as the picture of their dreams and their future. Poetic tributes paid to the Soviet Union by Subramania Bharati, Iqbal and later by Mahakavi Vallathol also fell in the same period.

In the second phase in the years 1936 to 1947, after the great mass struggles of the 2nd mass civil disobedience movement of the thirties, under the stress of massive repression and of the rich experience of the setbacks and achievements, the whole movement matured as a mighty united front of all anti-imperialist forces fighting for the country's independence and democracy. Its left wing composed of united working class organisation, the all India peasant's organisation and the mass movement in the princely states fighting against the feudal bastions of imperialism, became a powerful force giving the whole movement an orientation towards socialism and militant struggle.

Soviet Influence on Indian Plans

This united anti imperialist movement in India was advancing towards the final clash. In this phase, the historic achievements of the Socialist Soviet Union profoundly influenced our national movement and its left wing and became a factor in accelerating our country's advancement towards independence and in moulding its future image.

In the mid-1930s, on one hand, our people saw the system of imperialism entering into unprecedented economic crisis and transferring its burden to the dependent countries, spelling mass unemployment, retrenchment and wage cuts for the workers and employees and the mass ruin of the peasantry due to the catastrophic fall of commodity prices. On the other hand, they saw the spectacular achievements of the Soviet Union stabilising its socialist system, transforming the once backward Russia through socialist industrialisation and creation of a modern agriculture into a modern world power, bringing about a miraculous flowering of progress and culture among the once backward and oppressed peoples of its Asian regions.

This spectacular contrast exerted a revolutionary influence on our national movement, strengthening the socialist orientation of its leftwing. The popularisation of these achievements of the Soviet Union by the Communist Party, the working class and peasant mass organisations gave this orientation a widening mass base.

Under the influence of the experience of socialist planning for the industrialisation of the Soviet Union, the National movement established a planning commission under the initiative of Jawaharlal Nehru and Subhash Chandra Bose. The idea that independent India will have to build heavy and metallurgical industry through

Subhas Chandra Bose about Russian Revolution

Communism, for instance, is not a Western institution. Among the Khasis of Assam, to whom I have referred, private property as an institution does not exist in theory even today. The clan as a whole owns the entire land, I am sure that similar instances can still be found in other part of India and also in the past history of our country.

(Presidential address at Maharashtra Provincial Conference, Poona, 1928)

The most interesting phase of metamorphosis that has overtaken the British Empire is the fact that the High Priest of Imperialism, the arch-enemy of Indian nationalism, the sworn opponent of all forms of socialism, the British Prime Minister Winston Churchill has had to swallow all his former Imperialist pride and present himself at the gates of the Kremlin in Moscow".

(Broadcast from Azad Hind Radio on August 31, 1942)

the state sector and carry out agrarian reforms were already foreshadowed during these discussions under the influence of the Soviet experience particularly by Jawaharlal Nehru.

Secondly, the Soviet Union came forward as a world power – but a power of an entirely new type – a socialist power championing the cause of the freedom of the peoples, taking a stand against fascist aggressive drive towards war – which the western imperialist powers led by the Britain were promoting to turn against the Soviet Union.

The Indian freedom movement, under the initiative of Jawaharlal Nehru, who was profoundly influenced by the world movement of united front against fascism and war, began to take a stand against fascist aggression and war. This was expressed in the resolutions of the Indian National Congress. There were mass campaigns for supporting China fighting against imperialist Japanese forces. There were campaigns of supporting the democratic people of Spain, who were victims of fascist aggression, and there were campaigns for friendship with the Soviet Union. The Communist

Party and the mass organisations of workers and peasants played a prominent role in these campaigns. This projected the image of the Indian freedom movement as an anti-imperialist force, which stood against fascist aggression and for peace. It rendered support to Soviet Union and to countries fighting for their freedom.

Thirdly, the stupendous and heroic resistance of the Soviet Army and the entire Soviet people to the perfidious and monstrous aggression against their country by Hitlerite forces, and the noble and just war aims of liberation proclaimed by the Soviet leaders had a profound influence on India and its freedom movement. These two factors sustained its moral commitment to the anti-fascist cause and strengthened their conviction that India's liberation as well as the liberation of other people fighting for their freedom from imperialism and colonialism cannot be divorced from the victory of the socialist Soviet Union over fascism.

It is significant that this even took place in the context of the complicated conditions in India because of which Indian people could not participate in the anti-fascist struggle. British imperialists denied her freedom and power and instead launched leonine repression against the Indian people and the Quit India movement.

The heroic and self-sacrificing efforts of the Soviet people in completing their five years' plans of Socialist industrialisation and agricultural development, their successes in building up the military might of their country, coupled with their far-sighted initiative for building the world front against fascist aggression and war, ensured their historic victory over Hitler's fascism. The world saw for the first time in history how socialist people were capable of making stupendous sacrifices to defend their own country and their progressive socialist system and in doing so, created conditions for the liberation of other peoples and nations.

The heroic saga of Volgograd, the defence of Leningrad and the death-defying self-sacrifice of countless Soviet men and women, stirred our people to the depths and found expression in many poems and popular ballads in those days.

Thus, our own freedom struggle reached its revolutionary climax only after the war was brought to an end by the spectacular victory of the Soviet Union over Hitler's fascism. The outstanding role of the socialist Soviet Union in the victory in the anti-fascist war as a whole, the tremendous rise of its prestige and power, and the upsurge of liberation struggles of the dependent peoples of Asia unleashed by the defeat of Japan intensified the crisis of world imperialism as never before and sounded the death knell of colonialism.

Post-War Liberation Upsurge Sweeps

Our country was perhaps the first to achieve independence in this post-war liberation upsurge. Our independence was accompanied with imperialist-imposed partition, and our national democratic revolution remained unfinished. This was due to the weakness and division in the democratic forces, which failed to prevent the compromise made by the national bourgeois leadership who came to power after independence.

All the same, the government of independent India headed by Jawaharlal Nehru took the earliest initiative to establish diplomatic relations with Soviet Union. It was in a way the first significant step towards evolving an independent foreign policy of anti-colonialism, non-alignment and peace.

In fact even before India was proclaimed independent, Pandit Nehru, as the head of the interim government, had taken the initiative to convene an Asian Relations Conference to which Central Asian republics of the USSR were invited and an attempt was made to project the outlines of such a policy. It is true that an independent foreign policy of anti-colonialism, non-alignment and peace is a logical continuation of the international policies pursued by our freedom movement in second phase described above. But, that policy actually took shape and came to be recognised as such internationally in the early fifties after India itself was stabilised as an independent republic and only after the full impact of the historic victory of the Soviet Union over fascism came to be felt as a decisive shift of the balance of forces in favour of socialism and against imperialism.

This brings us to the third and the present phase of our national movement in which our people are fighting for economic independence, for social progress, and for advance to socialism. In this phase, the cooperation which began between India and the USSR, first in the international field, in the interest of peace and anti-colonialism (as in the case of Korean War) and later in the case of the Geneva agreement developed to cooperate in the economic field. This enabled India to get Soviet aid to develop heavy and key industries (such as iron and steel, oil, heavy forgings and machinery etc.) in the state sector and put her on the road to achieving economic independence.

It is necessary to state here with the utmost emphasis that the Soviet aid to India to establish the most modern iron and steel project in the state sector at Bhilai, was a turning point in our struggle for economic independence. It helped to break the blockade which the western imperialists sought to impose on our country trying to prevent it from developing modern iron and steel industry in the state sector.

'Mixed Economy' Unmixed Capitalism

The Soviet and Rumanian aid to India to develop its oil industry can enable us to rid our country of the exploiting grip of the western oil monopolies. Similarly, the heavy forgings and heavy machinery plant at Ranchi, several times sabotaged by reactionary elements, when completed can enable our country to build the plants for heavy industry indigenously.

That these possibilities have not yet been realised fully is mainly due to the fact that though the national bourgeois government took initiative to get this aid, but, at the same time, pursued the policy of what it called 'mixed economy'. Development in the realm of 'mixed economy' in reality was a policy of developing unmixed capitalism, of compromising with monopolists, foreign and Indian, and appeasing landlord and other vested interests. This policy in all its ramifications and in the course of three five year plans had led to a veritable crisis of our economy and development.

This economic crisis developed into a political crisis in the recent years and in our country the sharp struggle for the alternative paths, to which we referred earlier, is being intensified. In the context of the advance of the left and democratic forces in the last general elections and in its aftermath, the forces of monopoly reaction, in various combinations, are preparing to launch a counter-offensive, utilising all the weaknesses of the left and democratic forces and their failure to unite – a counter-offensive to dissent and suppress forces of democracy and progress and to give a whip hand to the forces of foreign imperialism, Indian monopoly and reaction. We are convinced that this counter-offensive can and must be defeated.

In our country, broad, progressive and democratic forces are coming together to celebrate the 50th anniversary of the Great October Socialist Revolution. It will be an occasion when our people will review the impact that the great event has made on our freedom struggle, and how the friendship and cooperation between the Socialist Soviet Union and India has been a factor in promoting progressive development in our country and the cause of peace and anti-colonialism in the world. The progressive course, which was initiated by this cooperation in the international arena and in the field of our internal development, must not be allowed to be eroded or subverted, but must be carried forward. That will be the message that will inspire all these celebrations.

Fifty years ago when the guns of Aurora announced the victory of this great event, and when the radio message proclaiming peace without annexations and indemnities and the right of the self-determination of nations went round the world, only a few believed that a turning point in human history had been reached wherein the era of the end of imperialism and colonialism and of the dawn of freedom had begun. The development of the last fifty years has brilliantly confirmed this prognosis.

Today the balance of forces has shifted decisively in favour of socialism, the socialist system is becoming more and more a determining factor in world politics, and the world revolutionary process is tremendously accelerated in the advanced capitalist countries and much more so in the oppressed and under-developed countries of Asia, Africa and Latin America.

Progressive humanity owes a debt of deep gratitude to the Soviet people, their Leninist Communist Party, its leaders and cadres who made the October Revolution and who later consolidated the victory of socialism following Lenin's behest, through stupendous sacrifices and struggles, defeating the machinations and attacks of the imperialists.

Thus the October Socialist Revolution and its creation, the Soviet Union from its initial triumph, its struggle for survival, its further consolidation, and its later historic victories and achievements, has all through been indissolubly linked with the world revolutionary process of which it was and remains a part and an advanced detachment at that. It is no wonder, therefore, that Lenin – the leader of the October Revolution and the architect of the Soviet Socialist State – was simultaneously the initiator and organiser of the Third Communist International (1919-43) which became the precursor of the present world communist and workers' movement.

The unity of the three main currents of the world revolutionary process – the process of transition from capitalism to socialism – constitutes the basic principle and the spirit of the international communist movement. These three currents are: the working class movement of the advanced capitalist countries – fighting for peace, democracy and socialism; the socialist system; and the national liberation movement of the oppressed peoples which today includes the fight of the working people of the newly independent countries for economic independence from imperialism and for advance to socialism.

It was the unity and joint action of these three currents and forces that in the early days of the revolution ensured the consolidation of the socialist victory. It was this unity and joint action that was the main content of proletarian internationalism and the basis of the world communist movement. Today when the general crisis of capitalism has entered the third stage – the stage of disintegration and collapse of the colonial system – when aggressive imperialism is fighting its last desperate battles in Vietnam and West Asia and elsewhere, the unity and joint action of these three main currents are more necessary than ever.

Lenin's Prophetic Words in 1923

In this connection we recall the prophetic words of Lenin written in 1923 stating that in the last analysis the final outcome of the struggle (meaning the world struggle for the victory of socialism) will be determined by the fact that Russia, India and China that account for the over-whelming majority of the world population of the globe, are today being drawn into the struggle for emancipation with extraordinary rapidity. Today 43 years after those words when that 'awakening' has already expressed itself in the victory of the great Chinese revolution and in the establishment of socialism there and in the emergence of the independent Indian republic and the strengthening of its democratic forces, we are faced with the regrettable developments in China that make a mockery of Lenin's vision. We find the Mao Tse-tung leadership of the People's Republic of China and its Communist Party engaged in escalating a monstrous campaign of slander against the Soviet Union and other socialist countries, in deliberate activities for splitting the unity of the socialist camp and for disrupting the world communist movement.

All this is being done in the name of fighting modern revisionism and furthering the alternative line of world revolution unilaterally proclaimed by the Mao Tse-tung leadership. In reality, it is the outcome of tendencies of petty-bourgeois, adventurist, great-power chauvinism and of the deification of the Mao-cult, that are a repudiation of communism, and which are today dominating in China and seeking to crush the forces of the working class fighting for socialism, for unity with the socialist camp and with the world communist movement.

The Communist Party of India and large sections of progressive and democratic forces in our country are with the Soviet Union and with other socialist countries, with the bulk of the world communist movement in their efforts to counteract the results of these splitting and disruptive activities. We pledge to restore the unity of the progressive and revolutionary forces of the world. We have no doubt that the spirit of the Great October Socialist Revolution, and its inspiring leader, Lenin – the spirit of unifying all the streams of the world revolutionary process in one mighty current will ultimately triumph ensuring the victory of the cause of socialism and peace the world over.

(*New Age Weekly*, November 6, 1967)

7

India's Freedom Struggle and the October Revolution

C. Achutha Menon

The Great October Revolution in Russia was a world-shaking event. It swept away in one mighty stroke the imperialist feudal order in Russia and ushered in a new social order and a new civilisation. At the same time, it acted as a harbinger of liberation to peoples all over the world who were subjected to colonial slavery.

In November 1917 the post-war mass upsurge in the struggle for freedom had not yet begun in India. But within less than two years, it did begin with the mighty events in the Punjab. On April 6, 1919, the all India protest hartal took place, the first ever in India's history, against the Rowlatt Act. Soon followed the terrible massacre of Jallianwala Bagh, the promulgation of martial law in Punjab and other acts of repression. Gandhiji assumed leadership of the national movement and brought the new weapon of Satyagraha and non-violent non-cooperation to the struggle. The whole country from the Himalayas to the southern seas was ablaze with the fire of anger and defiance against the 'leonine' violence of the British authorities.

All this obviously could not be ascribed to the influence of the Russian Revolution. Rather, this was part of the world-wide revolutionary upsurge following the crisis of world capitalism, of which the Russian Revolution itself was a part.

But the people of India could derive encouragement from the success of the revolution in Russia because it was a victory against czarist autocracy, the same kind of enemy which we in India had to fight. There was, therefore, genuine admiration in India among all classes for the Russian Revolution.

This found expression in songs, writings and speeches in the newspapers and periodicals published in different languages of India at that time. The great Tamil poet Bharati wrote a song in 1917 itself on "New Russia" in which he says that

Epoch-making revolution came to Russia
When Parasakthi cast her glance on her.

And that in the "Russia of peerless renown through the world there is neither slave nor fetters now". In later times innumerable Indian poets and writers have paid tributes to revolutionary Russia.

The one great feature of the Russian Revolution which appealed to all Indian nationalist, to whatever class or creed they belonged was the new state's policy towards nationalities. Lenin developed the theory of nationalities and it was embodied in the Decree on Nationalities which the new state proclaimed soon after coming to power.

Decree on Nationalities

The decree categorically declared that irrespective of the fact whether a territory was far from or near the metropolitan country, whether it was backward and illiterate or not, whether it was annexed recently or in the distant past, the territory of a distinct nationality had the right to self- determination and that the metropolitan country should grant it complete independence. This could be understood in India in no other sense than as a notice to quit to the British rulers.

To suppress the freedom movement, the government used not just naked repression but also false propaganda of the most vicious kind. They constantly used the bogey of 'Bolshevism' or 'Bolshevist conspiracy'.

When the third Afghan war broke out in 1919, the government tried to persuade the nationalist leaders to help the war efforts because it was supposed to be in the interest of national defence against the Bolshevik menace from across the border.

To the credit of the nationalist leaders it must be said that none of them were taken in by this ruse. Gandhiji declared categorically: "I have never believed in a 'Bolshevik menace' and why should any Indian government fear Russian, Bolshevik or any menace?" He refused to suspend mass action against the government in the name of defence.

The leaders of the Indian National Congress who were directing the struggle for freedom at that time could not be expected to accept the programme or forms of struggle adopted by the Russian Revolutionaries. For they belonged to a different class, they had a different background and different ideals.

Still they were in sympathy with the aims of the revolution in so far as it stood for ending autocracy and for the liberation of colonial peoples. But there were other elements in the Indian society who were inspired by the Russian Revolution in a different way. These latter eagerly hailed the ideas of workers and peasants rule and the methods of struggle adopted by the Bolsheviks to achieve it.

The working class in India had not at that time achieved the maturity to grasp these ideas. It was left to the Indian youth belonging to various revolutionary groups like the Anushilan, Jugantar, etc. in Bengal, the Mujahidins from several parts of North India, etc. to imbibe these ideas and work them out in their own way.

Socialist Ideas

Their number was not very large, but they played a significant role in the development of socialist ideas in the country, as well as the movements of the working class and the peasantry. These intrepid young men made the hazardous land journey across the Himalayan passes, first to Afghanistan and then to Russia, built up contacts with the Bolshevik leadership, got trained and came back to work in India.

They joined others who remaining in the country, working with the same aims. The two together spread over various parts of the country and it is from them that the Communist Party of India was subsequently born.

Such was the impact of the October Revolution in the aftermath of the First World War so far as India was concerned.

The picture was altogether different in the early thirties. In Russia, socialism had been consolidated by the successful completion of the First Five Year Plan. The entire capitalist world had gone through a big economic crisis, throwing hundreds of thousands of workers on the streets without work, keeping thousands of factories idle and destroying millions of tons of agricultural products because there were no purchasers.

India too, was caught up in the whirlpool of this terrific crisis, crushing the mass of the peasantry under the burden of debt because of the crash in the prices of their produce and depriving them of their land. Russia alone was unaffected by the depression.

Disobedience Movements

The civil disobedience movements of 1930 and 1932 had collapsed and there was a furious searching of hearts in all political circles. Thousands of young men, who came out of the jails dissatisfied with the Gandhian methods of struggle, were eagerly searching for a new path. They looked with hope and expectation at what was happening in the Soviet Union.

The new thinking was not confined to radical youth alone. Some among the senior leaders of the Congress had also begun to think in a new way. Foremost among them was Jawaharlal Nehru. Jawaharlal Nehru had, along with his father Motilal Nehru, visited the Soviet Union in 1928.

Although his visit was a short one, just 10 days, he was very impressed with what he saw in the Soviet Union. He was a keen student of world affairs and tried to figure out the concatenations of the various events taking place in different parts of the world with events in India.

He saw the Indian struggle for independence not as an isolated struggle, but as part of the worldwide struggle against imperialism. Imperialism during the thirties was fast assuming the shape of fascism. He also recognised the key role of the Soviet Union in the worldwide struggle against fascism.

Some of these thoughts he wished to share with his countrymen and for that purpose wrote the series of articles under the caption "Whither India" sometime in 1933. He put his conclusions more categorically and forcibly in his Presidential Address at the Lucknow session of the Indian National Congress in 1936 when he declared socialism as the only solution for the problems of India as well as of the world.

As stated earlier the old methods of struggle were felt to be inadequate to attain the goal of independence. Hence new methods were sought for. The importance of involving the workers and peasants in the struggle was recognised. It was felt that unless they came in a big way into the Congress and took part in the struggle, the struggle could not develop.

For that purpose the collective affiliation of workers and peasants organisations to the Congress was thought of. Nehru advocated it in the Lucknow Congress, but the Congress did not accept that suggestion.

However, mass organisations of workers and peasants were organised throughout the country and they, while fighting for their immediate demands, simultaneously fought for freedom. This gave a new sweep to the anti-imperialist freedom movement.

The independent class organisation of the workers was already there in the All India Trade Union Congress (AITUC). In 1936 was formed the independent class organisation of the peasants, All India

Nehru on October Revolution

Some glimpse we can have of this new civilisation in the territories of the USSR. Much has happened there which has pained me greatly and with which I disagree, but I look upon that great and fascinating unfolding of a new order and a new civilisation as the most promising feature of our dismal age.

If the future is full of hope it is largely because of Soviet Russia and what it has done, and I am convinced that, if some world catastrophe does not intervene, this new civilisation will spread to other lands and put an end to the wars and conflicts which capitalism breeds.

Presidential Address, Lucknow Congress, 1936

Kisan Sabha (AIKS). The students organised themselves in the All India Students Federation (AISF). The writers started their own organisation, the All India Progressive Writers Association in 1936.

All these different streams flowed into the main anti-imperialist stream thereby making it mighty and irresistible.

Meanwhile, all those who were socialist-minded within the Congress gathered together and formed the Congress Socialist Party in 1934. The Communist Party was still illegal, but its cadres were very active in the trade unions, Kisan Sabhas and other mass organisations as well as inside the Congress.

By 1936 many of the leaders of the party who were inside jail having been convicted in the Meerut conspiracy case were released and they began to take part in all these activities. In fact, the biggest ever anti-imperialist United National Front against imperialism emerged in India during the latter half of the thirties and lasted till the beginning of the Second World War.

Sentiments for Soviets

This United Front got disrupted partially as a result of the differing perceptions of the Indian National Congress and the Communist Party of India after Hitler's aggression on the USSR. While the

Communist Party recognised a change in the very character of the war, the war having changed into anti-fascist people's war, the Congress was not prepared to go to that extent.

But it is important to note that the mass sentiment in India in favour of the Soviet Union among all sections of the people, including the ranks of the Congress, was extremely strong. They all wished to see the Soviet Union win the war.

Therefore, even in the Quit India resolution of August 8, 1942, which called for a mass struggle against the British government in India, we find the following statement: "The All India Congress Committee is anxious not to embarrass in any way the defence of China and Russia, whose freedom is precious and must be preserved, or to jeoparadise the defence capacity of the United Nations".

The post-Second World War mass upsurge was the biggest ever witnessed by India. It far surpassed the mass upsurges of 1920, 1930 and even the Quit India movement of 1942.

It began with the countrywide protest demonstrations against the sentence awarded in the INA trials against three officers of the Indian National Army. In Calcutta, industry was completely paralysed, even the common citizens joined the demonstrations and pitched battles were fought in the streets between the people and the British army.

In 1946, there was the all India postal strike and uprisings in many native states like Kashmir, Hyderabad and Travancore. In Bengal the great Tebhaga struggle of the sharecroppers spread to more than 22 districts of the state and lasted several months. In the Punnapra-Vayalar uprising in October 1946, more than 300 workers were shot dead.

The post-war upsurge rose to its highest point in the strike of the Naval Ratings in Bombay in February 1946. The entire city came out in sympathetic demonstrations and about 200 people were shot down in the streets in the clashes that followed. It was clear that the alien regime was on its last legs, even its most trusted shield, the armed forces, having turned against it.

The British rulers realised that they could hold India no longer. That was how the transfer of power came in August 1947. Although freedom had been won, the struggle against imperialism did not end. Imperialism had in its armoury various devices by which newly independent countries could be subjected to their domination.

Through military alliances to surround recalcitrant countries, through so-called arms assistance and the system of military alliance, through terms of trade and exchange, diplomatic pressure and various other means, imperialism seeks to maintain its hold on a former colonial country and subject it to its will.

Imperialist Conspiracy

Although Britain had withdrawn into the background, having become a second-class power in the post-war period, the USA took its place and started to dictate policy. Our neighbour Pakistan became a pliant instrument of US policy, filling up arms borrowed from the US, thus posing a constant threat to India.

League against Imperialism

The Second Congress of the Comintern was an important precursor to the Brussels conference of the League Against Imperialism which was attended by Jawaharlal Nehru. Along with the Pan-African congresses, the Brussels conference was an early sign of the coming together of leaders of the anti-colonial struggle. This was continued by the Bandung conference in 1955 which eventually led up to the Non-Aligned Movement. Hence, the October Revolution influenced not just the Indian freedom struggle, but almost all of the anti-colonial struggles in the world. It was a challenge to those struggling against imperialism that while the basic nature of imperialism was to worsen the conditions of the masses of people, the ending of European rule had to uplift the condition of the masses, and not just the conditions of an elite few. Coming together of Africa and Asia against European imperialism and support from the Soviet Union was of great importance in this context.

In the new context India had to evolve a foreign policy of its own so as to safeguard its independence and resist pressures of imperialism. Such a policy was evolved by Jawaharlal Nehru, which has come to be known as the policy of non-alignment. Nehru, along with Gamal Abdel Nasser of Egypt and Marshal Tito of Yugoslavia, was the architect of that policy.

US Secretary of State John Foster Dulles denounced this policy as immoral, but the Soviet Union understood its significance and welcomed it. The Soviet Union recognised that the essence of non-alignment was anti-imperialism. In the new international situation that opened up after the end of the Second World War, the greatest danger to humanity was the constant threat of war that was posed by the ever increasing piling up of nuclear and other weapons of destruction.

The principal defence against this threat is the socialist system, in the world headed by the mighty Soviet Union. But this peace front has its firm ally in the community of non-aligned nations. This alliance is not only a guarantor of peace but also a firm ally of all peoples fighting colonial oppression, the system of apartheid or racial discrimination, etc.

Political freedom is only a shell; unless it is reinforced by economic content, it is nothing. India at the time of independence was a very weak country, industrially backward, dependent for its basic requirements like food, on other countries. All this had to be changed.

Rapid industrialisation was the only remedy for this. The so called western democracies were not willing to help India in this matter. So the USSR had to be approached and it readily extended all the help that was necessary.

Forty Years of Freedom

During the 40 years of independence, India has made very considerable progress in Industry with the help of the Soviet Union. In the production of steel and non-ferrous metals, in oil refining, in the manufacture of heavy machinery, in coal washing, in the manufacture of power production machinery etc. In fact, in every field that is required for laying the foundation of a self-reliant industrial economy the Soviet Union has come to the aid of India, making the latter self-reliant too through the process of aid. Seventy big Soviet-aided projects are now working in our country.

An important contribution to India's economic development is the idea of planning, that is to say, the idea that a country's economic development could be planned. This idea was obviously borrowed from the experience of the Soviet Union, its five year plans.

It may be remembered that in 1938 the Indian National Congress had appointed a national Planning Committee with Jawaharlal Nehru as Chairman and Prof. K.T. Shah as Secretary. The Committee prepared several interim reports, but the war broke out before the final report could be made and the task was left unfinished.

The government of independent India appointed a national Planning Commission which has the task of preparation and review of execution of the five year plans. Planning in an under-developed capitalist country like India is obviously different from planning in Soviet Union which is a socialist country.

But however partial and limited the function of planning in a capitalist economy may be, it is a valuable addition to the instruments available with the state in the cause of economic development of a backward country such as India. This also India owes to the example and experience of the Soviet Union.

Such in short has been the impact of the October Revolution on the course of our struggle for national independence and the development of free India.

(*New Age Weekly*, November 6, 1987)

8

Bhagat Singh and HSRA Heard the Call of the October Revolution

Bijoy Kumar Sinha

> The revolutionaries believe that the deliverance of their country will come through Revolution. The Revolution they are constantly working and hoping for will not only express itself in the form of an armed conflict between the foreign government and its supporters and the people, it will also usher in a New Social Order. The Revolution will ring the death knell of Capitalism and class distinctions and privileges. It will bring joy and prosperity to the starving millions who are seething today under the terrible yoke of both foreign and Indian exploitation. It will bring the nation into its own. It will give birth to a new State – a new social order. Above all, it will establish the Dictatorship of the Proletariat and will forever banish social parasites from the seat of political power... Here in India as in other countries in the past, terrorism will develop into the revolution and the revolution into independence –social, political and economic... We take this opportunity to appeal to our countrymen – to the youth, to the workers and peasants, to the revolutionary intelligentsia–to come forward and join us in carrying aloft the banner of freedom. Let us establish a new order of society in which political and economic exploitation will be impossibility... Let cowards fall back and cringe for compromise and peace. We ask not for mercy and we give no quarter. Ours is a war to the end – to Victory or Death. Long Live Revolution.

These are the words, clear and ringing, of the Manifesto of the Hindustan Socialist Republican Association under the caption, 'The Philosophy of Bomb', that was distributed all over the country in the beginning of 1930. It had to be issued as Gandhiji, with his doctrinaire faith in the efficacy of truth and non-violence, had through his writings in Young India and his speeches opened a sustained attack on the methods and ideas upheld by the revolutionaries.

Inspired by Liberation Struggles

Since the birth of their movement in the closing years of the nineteenth century in Maharashtra, since the period of Tilak and the martyrdom of the three Chapekar Brothers, Indian Revolutionaries had all long been drawing strength and inspiration from the

REDS BOMB INDIAN LEGISLATURE

BLAST FOLLOWING SHARP PARLIAMENTARY CRISIS CAUSES INJURY TO MANY

Sir George Schuster, Finance Member of Governor General's Executive Cabinet, Among Those Wounded by Explosion

SIR JOHN SIMON ESCAPES UNHURT

Socialist Literature Hurled With Bombs Into Crowded Chamber; Two Men Arrested Are Said to Have Confessed to Outrage

Associated Press

DELHI, India, April 8.—Two bombs exploded in the Indian legislative assembly today, sharp on the heels of a parliamentary crisis. Several persons were injured, causing a panic among the assemblymen.

THOSE INJURED

Among the injured was Sir George Schuster, finance member of the governor general's executive council. He, and the other injured were taken to a hospital. Sir John Simon, head of the crown committee for constitutional reform in India was standing with the president of the assembly when the explosion occurred, but was not injured.

Others inured were Sir B. Raghvendra, Mr. Shankar, Rao Dao, Mr. Dalal (seriously), I. N. Roy, deputy secretary of the Indian central committee, who was sitting in the officers' gallery. Roy bled profusely.

3 GOVERNMENT BENCHES WRECKED

Three government benches were torn to bits by the bombs.

Two men were arrested and were reported to have confessed after other bombs and pistols were found on their persons. They gave their names as Butukeswara Dutt, from Bengal, domiciled at Cawnpore, and Bgat Singh from Punjab.

Thrown into the crowded assembly room with two bombs was a red pamphlet entitled "Hindustan Socialist republican army" and signed by Balraj, honorary chief." Police who locked the doors to prevent the escape of the perpetrators had difficulty in restraining the crowd. V. G. Patel, president of the assembly had just ruled that discussion should not be allowed on the public safety bill until Saturday when the trial of alleged Com munist conspirators recently arrested should be concluded. The government contested Patel's power to bar discussion.

Sir John Simon had just completed a semester of investigation of facts and opinion which British authorities regard as the most important undertaking of its kind. The commissions's tentat.ve proposals may pave the way for a kind of su- tonomy for India.

India has had a strong nationalistic movement in recent years with intrusions of Communistic thought even more recently.

The work of the Simon commission, organized in 1927, chiefly to investigate India's capacity for self government was hindered from its start by nationalist opposition which took the form of partial strikes. The nationalists contended Indians should have greater representation on the commission.

Communistic agitation has occurred principally in the working districts. It was said in some quarters to have been responsible for the recent rioting at Bombay between Hindus and Pathans or Moslem Indians in which many were killed and injured.

An act of parliament in 1919 declared it the policy of the Britis[h] Empire to extend further powers of self administration with a view to ... realization of responsible govern-

News Report of Bhagat Singh and Batukeshwar Dutt, 8th April, 1929.

Bhagat Singh and HSRA

Bhagat Singh was born in 1907 and was 10 years old when the October Revolution happened. He first got politicised through the Gurudwara Reform movement and then witnessed the non-cooperation movement between 1920 and its end in 1922. Hence, he was the prime representative of a generation that was influenced by both; the ideas of the Russian Revolution and the idea of political freedom for their country. He was an intellectual and revolutionary, who not only had read a vast amount of literature, but became a martyr in the fight for independence, achieving immense popularity in the country. The Hindustan Republic Association, was formed in 1925 to achieve political independence and establish a Federated Republic of India. It was under the influence of Bhagat Singh, that they changed their name to the Hindustan Socialist Republican Association in 1928, and realised that political independence must also include economic freedom. They used acts of violence against the British, and were denounced as 'terrorists'. However, violence to them was only a means of publicising their revolutionary ideas. Indeed, their "Philosophy of the Bomb" pamphlet takes the criticism of their methods as an opportunity to educate people about the objectives of their movement.

revolutionary movement and the national liberation struggles all over the world. That is how it had broadened in its aims and methods during its different phases.

Starting as a movement of pure militant nationalism for complete independence of the motherland, it stood for a democratic republic during the years of the First World War, relying on the strength of the revolting Kisans and their brothers serving in the British army.

The Ghadar Party had about ten thousand members in India and abroad, was mainly of peasants. They had gone to America as emigrant labour or were spread in the countryside in Punjab. In the words of the famous Rowlatt Committee Report the party had "for its object the freedom of India from the British Raj by mutinying whereby the English were to be driven out of India and the country governed by the people themselves". The revolutionaries failed in their immediate objective but they paid a heavy price. About one hundred of them mounted the gallows, forty faced the firing squad, and over a hundred went to the Andamans sentenced to life imprisonment.

It was at this time, in October 1917, that the Russian Revolution triumphed in Russia. Heralding a new social order for the first time in world history, to champion the interest of the common men and women who till yesterday were the disinherited of the Earth, mere tools of labour to be exploited for the few.

The Indian revolutionaries received news of this victory with unbounded joy and set themselves to the study of its ideas and workings, as also establishing contacts with the leaders of the Soviet Union.

Baba Gurumukh Singh, a veteran leader of the Ghadar Party recently wrote that when the Ghadar Party attempt failed

> ....it made a heart searching and took stock of its strength and weakness and resolved to overcome them. In the meantime the October Socialist Revolution took place in Russia. The party was naturally interested in learning from their successful revolt and sent many of its members to Russia to study and imbibe their experience.

In India the difficulty was paucity of literature on Soviet Union. Books that were available were few and as for news, mostly garbled versions used to appear in papers as supplied by Reuter – a British news agency. Despite this, in the 1920s, from what material was available, the revolutionaries got substantial ideas about the fundamentals of scientific socialism and its successful application on the soil of Soviet Union. As I had also joined the ranks of revolutionaries during this period in Kanpur – an industrial town, I soon found myself in this new stream of thought and realised that our party known as Hindustan Republican Association working in UP, Bihar, Punjab and other parts of Northern India was moving towards a socialist goal.

One of our leaders was Sachindra Nath Sanyal who had been sent to the Andamans as a life term prisoner in 1915 and subsequently released in general amnesty at the conclusion of the war when reforms were announced by the government. He had contacts with M.N. Roy who was in Russia. Sanyal declared the new ideas in the party manifesto, "The Revolutionary", that was distributed all over India on a single day in 1925.

It stated:

> The immediate object of the revolutionary party in the domain of politics is to establish a Federal Republic of the United States of India by an organised and armed revolution… the basic principles of this Republic shall be universal suffrage and the abolition of all systems which make the exploitation of man by man possible. The revolutionary party is not national but international in the sense that its ultimate object is to bring harmony in the world and in this respect it follows the footsteps of the great Indian Rishis of the glorious past and of Bolshevik Russia in modern age. In the domain of economic and social welfare, the party will foster the spirit of cooperation in as large a scale as possible instead of private and unorganised business enterprises.

Sanyal was arrested and sentenced again to transportation for life in the Kakori Conspiracy Case of 1925. Four of the accused were hanged and my brother who had been attending the trial of the Kanpur Bolshevik Conspiracy Case in 1924 got a sentence of ten years, along with other accused who were sentenced from five to twenty years imprisonment. In this Kanpur case, Nalini Gupta, a revolutionary was one of the four accused in the dock. Ramacharan Lal Sharma, another revolutionary, could not be produced in court as he had escaped to Pondicherry.

It now fell on our shoulders, the members of the second rank of the party, to take up the reins of the party in our hands. We were in close touch with each other and spread in different centres all over the country as small groups. The very same centres also had groups of communists and we had contacts with them. In Lahore there was Bhagat Singh who was associating with Majid, Kedarnath Saigal and Sohan Singh Josh who were all later convicted in the

Meerut Conspiracy Case. He was also working on the editorial staff of *Kirti* headed by Josh.

In Kanpur, Ajoy Kumar Ghosh, who later became the General Secretary of the Communist Party of India had joined the party. We were class mates in school and college. Shaukat Usmani, after his release from jail following his conviction in the Kanpur Bolshevik Conspiracy Case of 1924 had also arrived here to renew his work. Ganesh Shankar Vidyarthi, Maulana Hasrat Mohani, Radha Mohan Gokulji were all supporting the socialist cause through their writings and public activities. They all knew us as revolutionaries and we had a close association with them through open and secret work.

Under the impact of the October Revolution there were rapid developments in the country. Labour was coming into its own. A number of dedicated communists were mobilising them. The powerful Girni Kamgar Union had been born in Bombay. But the country in general had to be awakened for an assault on British Imperialism. In the words of Ajoy Ghosh, as revolutionaries we felt that:

> ...as for the most important question, however, the question in what manner the fight for freedom and Socialism was to be waged, armed action by individuals and groups was to remain our immediate task. Nothing else, we held, could smash constitutionalist illusions, nothing else could free the country from the grip in which fear held it. When the stagnant calm was broken by a series of hammer blows delivered by us at selected points and on suitable occasions, against the most hated officials of the government, and mass movement unleashed, we would link ourselves with that movement, act as its armed detachment and give it a Socialist direction... And we looked upon ourselves as men who by their example would create the basis for the rise of a new leadership. Socialism for us was an ideal, the principle to guide us to rebuild society after capture of power.

Socialism was accepted as goal

It was at this time that Shaukat Usmani, who was leaving for the Comintern Meeting requested me at Kanpur to go along with him with some other comrades as representatives of the revolutionary party, to seek Moscow's aid for our programme. I consulted Bhagat Singh and we felt that it was not the opportune time. We should follow Usmani later after our party had arranged some militant actions that we had in view.

We now changed our party's name to Hindustan Socialist Republican Association to declare our faith in Socialism as our cause. In our central committee we also decided to propagate our socialist ideas from the scaffold and the forum of trials in which party men may get involved. We were convinced that it would prove effective to carry the message of revolutionary socialism to the mass of our people, to their minds and hearts in a speedy process. We also started Naujawan Bharat Sabha as our open platform.

It was in furtherance of this policy that bombs were thrown in the Central Assembly in April 1929 and a few months earlier the British police officer was killed in Lahore, who was responsible for Lala Lajpat Rai's death.

In the latter case, an HSRA leaflet posted in Lahore streets announced

> The murder of a leader respected by millions of people at the unworthy hands of an ordinary police official like J.P Saunders was an insult to the nation. It was the bounden duty of young men of India to efface it... Our objective is to work for a revolution which would end exploitation of man by man.[1]

---

1 It is commonly believed that Saunders was responsible for the death of Lala Lajpat Rai and therefore, HSRA revolutionaries decided to kill him. The fact as per the book mentioned below is that HSRA resolved to kill Mr. James Scott, Senior Superintendent of Police (SSP). For this purpose it was decided that Bhagat Singh and Shivaram Rajguru should attempt on the life of Mr. Scott with revolvers. Chandra Shekhar Azad, the absconder in the Kakori Conspiracy Case of 1925, was to direct the whole action and to work as a rear guard. Because of some confusion, the HSRA revolutionaries killed Mr. Saunders, another Assistant Superintendent of Police instead of Mr. Scott and one constable Chanan Singh, who was chasing them. (Sardar Bhagat Singh, Jatinder Nath Sanyal, May 1931, Later published by Bhagat Singh Foundation in 2006 edited by Prof. Jagmohan Singh.)

Declaring our new faith, Bhagat Singh in his last letter as his testament smuggled out of jail a few days before his hanging affirmed:

> Let us declare that the state of war does exists and shall exist so long as the Indian toiling masses and their natural resources are being exploited by a handful of exploiters... They may be purely British capitalist or mixed British and Indian or even purely Indian. It shall be waged ever with new vigour, greater audacity and unflinching determination till the Socialist Republic is established.

Earlier when bombs were thrown in the Assembly in April 1929, as protest against the Trade Dispute Bill and Public Safety Bill, both anti labour measures, HSRA pamphlets were also dropped. It declared "It is easy to kill individuals but you cannot kill ideas. Bourbons and Czars fell while revolutions marched triumphantly ahead". In the course of the trial that ensued, Bhagat Singh raised the slogan 'Long Live Revolution'. The government banned it but the nation defiantly took it up as the new battle cry expressing its urges and aspirations.

In the Lahore Conspiracy case some of the accused gave a statement refusing to recognise the court saying that:

> ...we feel that unless the whole social order is changed and socialistic society is established, the whole world is in danger of a disastrous catastrophe.

In the course of the trial we observed Lenin Day on January 27. Defying the court we put on red scarves, raised slogans like 'Long Live Socialist Revolution', 'Long Live Communist International', 'Long Live Lenin' and 'Down with Imperialism'. A cable for transmission was then handed over to the court. It ran "On occasion of Lenin Day we express our hearty congratulations on triumphant and onward march of Comrade Lenin's success for the great experiment carried on in Soviet Russia. We wish to associate ourselves with the world revolutionary movement. 'Victory to workers' regime', 'Woe to Capitalism', 'Down with Imperialism'."

These proceedings of the celebration were featured in the *Tribune* and other newspapers. The Naujawan Bharat Sabha was carrying on socialist propaganda all the time on similar lines. The HSRA in another manifesto distributed in Lahore Congress gave a warning:

> The leaning of certain politicians in favour of Dominion Status shows clearly which way the wind blows. Indian capital is preparing to betray the masses into the hands of foreign capitalism and receive as a price of this betrayal, a little share in the government of the country....

For his sacrifice and daring and above all his socialist thoughts expressing the dreams and hopes of the people, Bhagat Singh became the beloved son of the entire nation. Pattabhi Sitaramayya, the officials historian of the Congress wrote in 1931 that "it is no exaggeration to say that at that moment Bhagat Singh's name was as widely known all over India and was as popular as Gandhi's".

Other HSRA members Rajguru and Sukhdeo mounted the gallows in Lahore jail along with Bhagat Singh; Chandra Shekhar Azad died fighting a pitched battle with police in Allahabad. Bhagawati Charan Vohra, writer of 'Philosophy of Bomb', became a martyr on the banks of the Ravi testing bombs for the escape of Bhagat Singh, Jatin Das passed away in an epic group hunger strike at Lahore and Thakur Mahabir singh defying the authorities, in distant Andamans, breathed his last in a mass hunger strike. They were all crusaders for the socialist cause. Through their chosen death, they all delivered the message of socialism - of a new life of genuine Equality, Freedom and Happiness to the teeming millions of their dear and vast motherland.

(*New Age Weekly*, November 5, 1967)

Bhagat Singh

9

Revolution of 1917 and its Impact on Indian Women

Hajrah Begum

Not till the late 1920s did the ordinary Indian women come to know of the historic events that had taken place in Russia in 1917. Almost for ten years imperialism prevented any but the most rabid anti-Soviet propaganda – calling the new state anti-religion, anti-god, destroyer of families and morality – from reaching the people. It was not till 1927 and 1928 that the truth began to filter through.

Two things happened by that time. The early revolutionaries who had gone abroad and been in touch with the Bolshevik Party of Russia on their return to India not only smuggled literature about Marxism and Communism but also reports of the heroic contribution of women revolutionaries to the success of the Russian Revolution.

Spirit of Revolution

Inspired by the examples of the sacrifice of those great Russian women, Indian women and young girls began to be associated with various underground revolutionary groups in this country. Thus even girls in their teens like Kalpana Dutt of Chittagong Armoury Raid Case who were active with secret organisations learned to revere the name of the great Lenin and to think of the October Revolution as the greatest example of the revolt of an entire people against tyranny and oppression.

Then a number of these 'terrorists' were rounded up and put under detention or sentenced to heavy terms of imprisonment. Their comrades saw to it that they were provided whatever literature was available at that time. Thus a good number of former 'anarchists', terrorists and revolutionary young girls came to study the events of 1917 behind bars.

Bengal was at the time the hotbed of revolutionary fervour and it was but natural that the first women to come over to communism should be from Bengal. Suhasini Ganguli for instance, commonly known as 'Putudi' was one of those who studied Marxist literature in jail and was one of the first to join the Communist Party. Kamala Chatterji was already well known as a revolutionary when she was arrested, and through her study and conviction joined the Communist Party. Indu Sudha Ghosh was a detenu from the Mymensingh group who also joined the Communist Party as did Shanti Ghosh after she became Shanti Das.

Other detenus, who did not join the Communists but became familiar with communist literature and the history of the Russian Revolution were Bimal Protiva Debi, Kalyani Bhattacharya, Indumati Sinha, etc.

Apart from the Bengal groups there were women working with Bhagat Singh and other revolutionaries in Punjab, United Provinces and Delhi. They were also in touch with what was happening in the Soviet Union and had great respect for Lenin and the success which the Bolshevik Party had achieved under his leadership. Amongst them the names of Durgawati Vohra (commonly known as Durga Bhabhi) of the Saunders Shooting Case and Parkashvati Paul stand out.

Side by side with the underground current was the second trend noticeable in the country. At about the same time militant trade unions were being organised in Bombay, Calcutta, Ahmedabad and Kanpur under the leadership of the newly formed Communist

Party. Speakers at meetings organised by these unions narrated at length the achievements and successes of the Soviet Union where in 1917 the working people, men and women had captured power.

The impact of such propaganda on the working women was astounding. Thousands and thousands of women themselves workers or belonging to the families of workers flocked to these meetings, joined the trade unions, marched in demonstrations and took to their hearts the flag with the hammer and sickle and the cry of 'Long Live the Revolution'.

Veteran Communists recall with pride the fact that in the historic strike of the Girni Kamgar Union in 1928 women workers were in the forefront organising pickets, collecting strike funds and facing police brutality valiantly and courageously. The activities of the Calcutta Chatkal Mazdoor Union called forth a similar response.

This tremendous fervour of the working class threw up a new type of woman trade unionist. Ushatai Dange was one of the first to plunge into the struggle of the working class and lead its militant struggle. Others who entered the field under the banner of the Communist Party were Suhasini Nambiar, Minakshi Sardesai, and others.

Women as Trade Unionists

Militant trade unionism found its reflection in the stand of also such women trade unionists who remained outside the fold of the

Durgawati Vohra (Durga Bhabhi)

Capt. Lakshmi Sehgal

Preetilata Waddedar

Kalpana Dutta

Chittagong Armoury Raid

Preetilata Waddedar and Kalpana Dutta

On April 18 1930, a heroic deed occurred, now the subject of unending legends — The Chittagong Armoury Raid. The raid was organised under the leadership of the great Surjya Sen, the leader of the Indian Republican Army, Chittagong Branch. In a time when it was widely believed in the revolutionary circles that the yoke of British Empire could only be thrown away with the help of some outside power, Surjya Sen's group tried to exhibit that this was not true. "For this their plan was open armed conflict, widespread planned action to raid the government armoury and seize arms, cut communications and prevent the Government from getting reinforcements from other parts of India and attack not individual Europeans but raid the club where they were to be found in numbers and give battle. For a week Chittagong would be free!" After the Armoury raid and the Jalalabad hill battle, in which over 100 British soldiers were killed and their arms were taken away by revolutionaries, severe persecution followed. For over two years, many revolutionaries were caught and prosecuted, transported for life and executed — most of them in their teens. But despair and frustration was something unknown to the invincible hearts of those revolutionaries. They planned another series of attacks on British establishments.

Preetilata Waddedar was one of the young comrades of the party. On September 24, 1932, under the leadership of young

Preetilata, eight comrades of the party attacked the "Pahartali Railway Club", a known gathering place for British officials. The signboard of the club read "Dogs and Indians Not Allowed". According to British Officials 13 were severly wounded and one was killed. All the 8 comrades came back unharmed but Preeti never came back. She consumed Potassium Cyanide, her shirt soaked in blood from a wound.

Kalpana Dutta was a member of the party. She came in contact with the revolutionaries in 1929, when she was barely 16. She accompanied the group till the very end braving arrests, police repression and bullets. She was given life imprisonment and Surjya Sen was sentenced to death. After a popular movement for the release of political prisoners, she was released in 1939 having served seven years in different jails. She joined the CPI later and worked extensively for relief in the great Bengal famine on party's call, when CPI was running 700 community kitchens, feeding 1,17,000 famine stricken destitutes. She worked all her life for the upliftment of the downtrodden. In 1943, she married CPI's then General Secretary P.C. Joshi. She breathed her last in 1995. She kept her attachment with people's movements and the party intact all her life.

Communist Party but who had firm faith in the victory of the working class and looked to the Soviet Union for guidance and inspiration in the struggle. Sudha Roy, Maitreyee Bose, Ambutai Bahere, Prabhavati Das Gupta were some of those who under the leadership of parties such as the Labour Party, Bolshevik Party, RCPI or Royists devoted their time to political work.

By the beginning of the thirties, students returning from Europe started study groups and discussions based on Soviet literature. Inside jail the study of Marxism took the form of regular schools and classes and a number of women who had participated in the freedom movement under the leadership of Gandhiji now openly took the stand for socialism.

Among the leading women of the socialist groups who clearly demarcated themselves from the Communists while standing by the principles of socialism and looking to the Soviet Union as the one country where socialism had triumphed, were Kamladevi Chatto – padhyay, Maniben Kara, Satyavati Devi and Poornima Banerji.

Inspiration for Social Reforms

An important aspect of the impact of the Russian Revolution which cannot be overlooked is the deep influence it had over the movement for women's rights as a whole.

In the pre-World War I period, Indian social reforms had turned to Europe for inspiration regarding women's education and social advancement though at the same time they dreaded the effect of such westernisation on Indian society.

When Indian women who had been agitating for women's rights came to know of the successes achieved by the Communist Party of the Soviet Union, especially in the eastern Soviet Republics, in freeing women from feudal bondage and social inferiority, teaching and training them to take their place side by side with the men in every walk of life – factories, schools, hospitals, colleges, army and legislature – they received tremendous encouragement. Here was a country whose women under conditions similar to those prevailing in India had in a short space of time accomplished what women of far more 'advanced' countries were still struggling to achieve!

As Lenin said in 1919,

> Not a single democratic party in the world, not even the most advanced bourgeois republic, has done in tens of years a hundredth part of what we did in the very first year we were in power. We really razed to the ground the infamous laws placing women in a position of inequality, restricting divorce and surrounding it with disgusting formalities, denying recognition to children born out of wedlock, enforcing a search for their fathers, etc., laws numerous survivals of which, to the shame of the bourgeoisie and of capitalism, are to be found in all civilised countries.

Rameshwari Nehru, pioneer of the movement for women's rights speaking as early as 1929 said:

The fact of women's subjection, in a more or less acute form in all regions and in all times, stands out prominently through history. Now there is a revolt against it. Women are not satisfied with being merely the subjects of men's actions. They claim to have a hand in the administration of their affairs. The evergrowing number of women serving in the legislative and executive bodies in the Western countries is a monument of their success and it is noteworthy that their number is greater in the countries which are inclined towards socialism or towards the recognition of the rights of individuals opposed to the privileges of classes. In Russia women are serving on all administrative bodies.

The Soviets brought us Salvation

One can get a glimpse of the immediate impact of the October Revolution on women through Clara Zetkin's experience with Muslim women at the Muslim Women's Club of Tiflis, founded in 1923 by the Communist Party. The first thing which struck her in 1926, when she visited the club, was the sight of a large number of Muslim women, "all of whom had discarded the veil". Clara Zetkin narrated the outburst of joy of one of those women in the club. She spoke: "How was our life before the revolution, our fathers sold us like young lambs when we were hardly ten or twelve years old — sometimes even younger. Our husbands demanded our affection and love, even when they seemed to us revolting. When our husbands were in the mood for it, they beat us with clubs or whips. We had to serve them day and night like slaves. When they grew tired of us, they told us to go to hell. They rented us out as mistresses to their friends... No Mullah came to our aid when we were in need..." Then she continued: "But now, my dear sisters, how everything has changed! The revolution arrived like a mighty thunderstorm. It has smashed injustice and slavery.... The Soviets brought us salvation. Eternal gratitude to them". Clara Zetkin, while narrating this incident, commented: "The economic basis of the old patriarchal family has shattered... In the literal sense of the word, the Revolution came as a redeemer to the Muslim women of Tiflis."

(From the article October Revolution: Towards Women's Equality, by Gargi Chakravartty, Mainstream Weekly, November 06, 2017)

Later, in 1932 Rameshwari Nehru visited the Soviet Union and ever afterwards remained a warm admirer of its stand regarding equality and freedom of women.

Sarojini Naidu, another great figure in the struggle for women's advancement, also maintained close contact with the events taking place in the Soviet Union through several close friends and relatives who were known Communists. She also appreciated the great strides made by women of the Eastern Soviets in freeing themselves from feudal bonds.

Abiding Interest

Aruna Asaf Ali, another pioneer of the Indian women's movement for equal rights and winner of the Lenin Peace Prize, vividly recalls the tremendous impression made on her when she first learnt of the happenings of October 1917 through reading the book "Ten Days That Shook the World".

Aruna Asaf Ali read all that was available about the Russian Revolution and the Communist Party of the Soviet Union though it was not till many years later that she visited the Soviet Union. "Most of the leading women of the freedom movement", she recalls, "had a keen interest in the progress made by women of the Soviet Union and received encouragement from the successes registered there".

(*New Age Weekly,* November 5, 1967)

Aruna Asaf Ali

Aruna Ganguly was born in 1909 and spent her childhood years at a catholic school in Nainital. After resisting her parents'

attempts to have her married, she left home at a young age to earn a living as a teacher at a girls' school in Calcutta. At 18 years, she married a Muslim barrister 20 years her senior, Asaf Ali, despite opposition from her family. She took a keen interest in politics, attending political meetings that caused her to come into contact with Congress leaders like Jawaharlal Nehru and M.K. Gandhi. Aruna came into her own as a leader during the Quit India movement. It was her act of defiance in unfurling the national flag at Bombay that virtually marked the inauguration of the movement. Following the arrest of all Congress leaders in 1942, Aruna went underground to guide the movement. Despite being hunted by the police, she acted with great courage, visiting major cities to talk and build unity with political leaders. She made heroic efforts to refocus the movement after its collapse in 1944. Despite being an ardent follower of Gandhi, she criticised his support to the British in their war effort and his condemnation of the violence of freedom fighters. In the post-independence era, Aruna's radical views came into conflict with the Congress, and she joined the Socialist Party in 1948. Breaking away from it she formed the Left Socialist Group in 1950 and worked actively with the trade union movement. The group merged with the CPI, and Aruna served as a member of the Party's Central Committee for a brief period.

Godavari Parulekar

Godavari Parulekar (1907-1996) was a freedom fighter, writer and social activist. She was the niece of Gopal Krishna Gokhale and began her social and political work by joining Servants of India Society. In 1939, she and her husband Shamrao Parulekar joined the Communist Party of India. They helped in organising the first anti-war strike of textile workers in Mumbai. Later she joined the All India Kisan Sabha and established it's Maharashtra Branch in 1945. Godavari and Shamrao led the Warli Adivasi Revolt in Umbergaon, Dahanu and Palghar Taluks during 1945 and 1947. This revolt was an integral part of the pre-Independence peasant upsurge against landlordism that included glorious struggles like Tebhaga, Telangana and Punnapra Vaylar revolt. After the split, she joined CPI (M) and in 1968, she became the National President of the All India Kisan Sabha, the only woman to hold this post.

Part 3

Post-Independence Period

On 29th March, 1943, four young comrades associated with Communist Party of India were hanged in Kannur Central Jail in the Malabar region of Kerala. Their names were Com. Kunhambu, Com. Chirukandan, Com. Aboobacker and Com. Appu. They were held responsible for conspiring against the British Empire and murder of a constable in Kayyur. The intention of this action was to suppress the growing strength of communists in the Malabar region. Com. Krishna Pillai, Com. EMS Namboodiripad, Com. A.K. Gopalan and others were leading the movement. Before the hanging was to take place, Com. P.C. Joshi, then General Secretary of the Communist Party and Com. P. Sundarayya, along with P. Krishna Pillai visited them. It was an emotional meet, but the jailed comrades who were going to be hanged within days, assured the leaders that they were honoured to sacrifice their lives for the party and for the freedom of the country.

Introduction (Part 3)

Two debilitating consequences of colonialism, both of which are well documented, were the 'drain of wealth' from India and its 'deindustrialisation'. India served as a source of raw materials, and also as a market for British industrial goods. British colonialism destroyed the indigenous weavers and artisans in India which caused a shift back to agriculture. Those who were displaced from their traditional livelihoods found employment in the infamous plantations as coolies and worked in conditions of semi-slavery. On leaving, the British partitioned India in two parts and left a society with 84 per cent illiteracy and 90 per cent poverty. India was used primarily to serve the economic interests of the British empire, which was most vividly brought out in the various famines that happened under British colonialism. Despite the availability of food grain, arguments about 'free market' were used to export it even as people starved in India. Along with the economic devastation, came the cultural devastation. There was an attempt to create a bureaucracy that would serve British interests and be educated in British culture, a class of men who were Indian in the colour of their skin but British in manners.

As a consequence, independent India had to undertake economic, cultural and political reconstruction, which was influenced by the Russian Revolution and the experience of the Soviet Union. Most leaders of the anti-colonial struggle in India called for some form of socialism to lift the conditions of the masses in the country.

Political reconstruction in India had two aspects. One task was to restructure the domestic institutional frame and the other was to position India's stand in the complex world political scene. The Constitution of India came into effect on January 26, 1950 replacing the Government of India Act, 1935 as the governing document of India. The draft Constitution reproduced a good part of the provisions of erstwhile Government of India Act, but the Constitution borrowed many redeeming features from other sources. The ideal of justice, elaborated in the Preamble of the Constitution, clearly reflected the impact of socialist ideology on the thinking of those who drafted the Constitution. Soon after, the government engaged itself in abolishing the princely states and joining those territories in the Indian Union. The states in federal India were reorganised on linguistic basis. The roots of democracy were deep and strong in the immediate post-independence period. The feudal and semi-feudal institutions were abolished unequivocally. The land reforms and trade union acts defined the place of peasantry and working class in the country's polity and society.

Internationally, India stood for world peace, justice and sovereignty of the newly independent country. Jawaharlal Nehru was one of the main architects of the Non-Aligned Movement (NAM) and he succeeded in positioning India as a prestigious nation heading the third world.

An important part of socialism was the planning of the production and distribution of goods. The precursor to economic planning in independent India was the Karachi Congress in 1931 where it was resolved that the state shall own or control key industries, services, railways, etc. A national Planning Committee was set up by the Congress party under its then president Subhash Chandra Bose who appointed Jawaharlal Nehru as its president in 1938. Both of these leaders were very impressed by the economic development of the Soviet Union. Economic planning continued to be an important part of the policy of independent India.

The reconstruction of a national culture was another important aspect which was extremely complicated in India because of its immense diversity in culture. It is worth mentioning the important role of mass organisations set up by the Communist Party in carrying out this reconstruction. These mass organisations based their art and literature in the life and struggle of ordinary people in the period after colonialism.

In carrying out this reconstruction, the leaders of the anti-colonial struggle were not just struggling against history, but were also struggling against continuing efforts of neo-colonialism by imperialist countries. Imperialism continued after the colonies gained their independence under the guise of economic aid, treaties, coups, interventions and sometimes by direct war. Hence, the anti-colonial leaders recognised that they would have to come together in unity against imperialism. This was the spirit of the Non-Aligned Movement, the World Peace Movement, of the Afro-Asian Writers' Conferences, all of which found support from the Soviet Union.

The first article here is by Ajoy Ghosh. It is a brief article but it goes over many aspects of the post-colonial period including the Peace Movement, the Non-Aligned Movement, economic planning and the political scene. The article by B.T. Ranadive is much more detailed and goes into the economic aspects of India's post-independence period. It elaborates with statistics the economic dependence of post-colonial countries on the imperialist world and how the imperialist world exploited this dependent relationship. Similarly, he uses elaborate statistics to illustrate positive support given by the Soviet Union and other socialist countries to help the post-colonial countries to stand on their own feet. The next article is by Rajeev Saxena. It gives a nice summary of the impact of the October Revolution on literature though it focuses only on Hindi literature. However, it makes an interesting point about the relationship between literature and revolution. It is supplemented by a separate note elaborating additional important features of cultural reconstruction.

Finally, we have added three articles on the Russian Revolution and its relevance written after the fall of the Soviet Union. The article by A.B. Bardhan brings the significance of the October Revolution to the current period. It speaks of the coming of the neo-liberal era and the forces of reaction after the fall of the Soviet Union, but emphasises that people have to start afresh and discuss the strength and mistakes of the Soviet Experiment. We have to learn lessons and engage ourselves once again with the task of moving forward towards Socialism in this era. The article by D. Raja is on the importance of understanding and applying the principles of socialism today. It underlines Lenin's theses on nationalities as it was applied in the Soviet Union.

The last article by Shameem Faizee examines the current hegemony of finance capital and describes the common features of its political consequences in various parts of the world. It also briefly describes the political situation in India today and quotes from the political resolutions of the Communist Party of India.

The world political scene as is emerging in the present conjuncture is in a context when political interventions from an alternative socialist camp are marginal. If the Soviet Bloc had remained, whatever its imperfections, the world political scene would have been different though we cannot say what form it would have taken. The collapse of the Soviet Bloc has unleashed an unfettered imperialist and capitalist order whose consequences we are facing today. It has also created a vacuum which must be filled with a new imagination of socialism. In this crisis of finance capital, we must not only consider the specific conditions that require socialism in our own society, but consider them in the context of the world political situation. India has always played an important role in the world, and its anti-colonial struggle has influenced many liberation struggles in Africa and Asia. As we imagine and create a new future, the history of the Russian Revolution and the Indian freedom struggle must guide us and we must remain committed not only to our own working class but to all oppressed people.

Soviet experts at the Bhilai Steel Plant construction site in India, 1962.

The agreement for constructing Bhilai plant was signed with the Soviet Union in 1955 after Indian Prime Minster Jawaharlal Nehru visited Magnitogorsk, or Magnitka, the capital of Russian iron and steel works.

The story of Konstantin Khabarov (1925–1993), a famous blast furnace operator of the Magnitogorsk steel plant, who was involved in the launching of blast furnaces at both Bhilai and Bokaro, is revealing. In his memoirs shared with Magnitogorsk Metal newspaper back in 1980s, Khabarov recalled being sent to Bhilai along with three other engineers to solve a major problem that occurred as result of a mistake of inexperienced workers.

"Due to some mistake the cast iron solidified in the furnace. It was too serious. The British, German and US experts advised to dismantle and rebuild the blast furnace. It would have taken at least a year to do it", he said.

The team of Russian operators spent days and nights at the plant and did the impossible: in twelve days the dead blast furnace was operational. Since then Khabarov was called "the Volcano Man" among Bhilai workers.

(Source: https://www.rbth.com/economics/2014/08/22/bhilai_steel_plant_chhattisgarhs_icon_of_indo-russian_cooperation_37741)

10

Long Live October Revolution

Ajoy Ghosh

On November 7, 1957, people all over the world will celebrate the Fortieth Anniversary of one of the greatest events in human history – the October Revolution which ushered in a new era, the era of Socialism, the era of the transition from class society to classless society.

Epoch making in every respect has been the transformation that has taken place in the USSR in these 40 years. The remaking of nature over a vast area comprising one-sixth of the world, the use of atomic energy for the benefit of man, the first major step towards the conquest of space symbolised in the launching of the man-made earth's satellite – these are a few events which amply demonstrate to what height man's creative endeavour can rise once it is freed from the thralldom of capitalism.

Translating into reality, under the leadership of the Bolsheviks headed by V.I. Lenin, the noblest dream of man and the immortal ideas of Marx and Engels, the USSR, born out of the October Revolution, proved conclusively that socialism is not a utopia.

It gave a deathblow to the belief sedulously fostered by the exploiters that the toiling people are incapable of governing the country.

It infused courage and confidence into the proletariat of all countries and made it conscious of its creative powers and of its historic role as the builder of a new society.

It showed that at the root of the major problems that confront mankind today – economic crisis and distress, mass unemployment and destitution, colonial slavery and racial persecution, conflicts between countries and the ever-present menace of war – lies not the innate evil in man but the division of society into exploiters and exploited and that this division can be ended not by appeals to the exploiters and efforts to change their heart but only through the conquest of power by the exploited masses led by the working class and the rebuilding of society on a new basis.

Massive Successes

The massive successes of the USSR in every sphere and its role in the war against fascism created the condition for one-third of humanity to take to the path of socialism. The might of the USSR acted as the shield of the new world against the frustrated efforts of imperialists to undertake intervention on a big scale. The help rendered by the USSR enabled the countries of People's Democracy to rebuild their economy.

No event, as is now recognised, both by friends and by enemies of socialism, has so decisively influenced the course of history during the last 40 years as the victory of the October Revolution.

No phenomenon has produced such a profound impact on the mind of man as the rapid transformation of a once backward country into the second industrial power of the world, the spectacular advance of the Soviet people in the sphere of science and technology, art and literature, the abolition of unemployment, destitution and cultural backwardness.

No country has made such a great contribution as the USSR to the struggle for the defence of peace, and the establishment of relation of friendship and amity between states, and so resolutely upheld the right of every nation to be free and sovereign.

Hence, it is but natural that the Fortieth Anniversary of the Great October Socialist Revolution is an occasion of joyous celebration not merely for the peoples of the USSR and the socialist world but for the whole of progressive mankind.

Special Significance

For the people of India who having won national freedom are striving to build a new life, who, together with the USSR, the Chinese People's Republic and other peace loving states are defending the cause of world peace; the Fortieth Anniversary of the October Revolution has a special significance.

Few were the people in India who, in the days when the revolution took place, understood clearly what had happened. The precise nature of the economic transformation which Socialism implies was yet unknown to Indians. But some features of the Revolution stood out sharp and clear.

First, czarist autocracy and despotism which held Russia in its grip for centuries had ended forever.

Secondly, the oppressed nations of Russia had won independence and were free to secede if they desired.

Thirdly, the new Soviet State had renounced all the privileges which the czarist Russia had wrung from its weak Asian neighbours and established new relations with them on the basis of equality. These were features full of immense significance for the people of Asia.

"The declaration of the rights of the peoples of Russia over the joint signature of Lenin and Stalin", wrote K.N. Panikkar, former Indian Ambassador to China, "proclaimed the equality and sovereignty of the peoples of Russia and the rights of the peoples of Russia to freedom and equality of national minorities. This was indeed an explosive statement and all the nations of Asia struggling for freedom heard it with a new hope." (*Asia & Western Dominance*, p. 250, 1953)

The imperialist rulers of India also noted the phenomenon. The Report on Indian Constitutional Reforms, signed by Mr. Montague, the Secretary of State for India, and Lord Chelmsford the Viceroy, issued on April 22, 1918, stated with evident regret that the Revolution had "given impetus to Indian political aspiration".

In the period of political and economic mass upheavals that swept over the country after the First World War, the British rulers faced a situation of greater peril than they had ever known since the Great National Revolt of 1857. In this period also arose the mass trade union movement embracing lakhs of workers. India witnessed the first stirrings of Socialist ideas, ideas as yet lacking clarity and precision but inevitably gravitating towards Marxism-Leninism under the impact of the October Revolution.

Despite heavy obstacles, despite repeated setbacks, despite periods of lull, the process that began in those tumultuous years has gone forward. India has broken the chains of colonial slavery and has become a major factor in the world arena, with immense prestige and authority. The working class of India has emerged as an independent force and is playing an increasingly important role in the life of the country.

The Communist Party has grown to the stature of the second party in the country, the main party of opposition in the Indian Parliament, with 12 million votes in the last general elections and leading the government in the state of Kerala. The ideas of the October Revolution have won millions of adherents, thereby refuting the thesis that Marxism-Leninism has become outmoded and has no validity for our country.

Contacts with Soviet Union

Together with these developments, the walls that the imperialists had raised between the people of our country and the country of victorious socialism have gradually crumbled.

As early as 1928 when the Soviet State, having overcome the ravages of war, of foreign intervention and civil strife, was laying the foundation of the new society and the possibility of building socialism in a single country was still being stubbornly disputed

Development of free India — a missed opportunity

The parliamentary elections of 1951-52, 1957 and 1962 were won by Congress Party with overwhelming majority, getting 364, 379 and 361 seats respectively. In all the three elections, CPI emerged as the main opposition party, albeit with small number of seats: 16, 27 and 29 and small percentage of vote share. Stalwart like S.A. Dange, A.K. Gopalan, Indrajit Gupta, Hiren Mukerjee, Bhupesh Gupta, Renu Chakravarti, P.K. Vasudevan Nair, Homi Daji and others were members of parliament and significantly contributed to important debates. In 1957, CPI won the assembly election in Kerala state and made world history. It was the first time in the world that an elected communist government assumed office. The communist government in Kerala immediately introduced radical agrarian reforms and reforms in educational institutes. The vested interests put up a strong opposition to the government which ultimately resulted in central government dismissing the communist government and imposing President's Rule in the state.

So far as other states were concerned, the land reforms only succeeded in abolishing Zamindari system, but land did not reach the tillers of land. In 1960s, with Green Revolution, the feudal lords were replaced by resource rich powerful capitalist farmers.

At the same time the Bourgeois government skilfully prevented the industrial working class from assuming its due place in the nation-building project. The All India Trade Union Congress (AITUC) was split and INTUC was formed in 1947. The trade union acts provided job security and other privileges to the industrial working class, but at the same time weakened the trade union's powers to fight for workers' rights and oppose the employers and state.

Comrade Gangadhar Adhikari in his article in previous section mentioned that in the immediate post independence period, there was a sharp struggle in deciding the future path. The major contention was will the country move towards completion of democratic revolution and advance to socialism, or will it continue with development of capitalism and growth of monopoly spelling untold sufferings to the working people and danger to country's independence.

Unfortunately, the nation building project missed the opportunity and the country fell into the trap of capitalist development which led to neo-liberalism and complete political and economic subservience to imperialist forces.

by many, Pandit Jawaharlal Nehru, after his visit to the Soviet Union wrote:

> Russia thus interests us because it may help us to find some solution for the great problems which face the world today. It interests us especially because conditions there have not been and are not even now very dissimilar to conditions in India. Both are vast agricultural countries with only the beginnings of industrialisation and both have to face poverty and illiteracy. If Russia finds a satisfactory solution for these, our work in India is made easy… It is right, therefore, that India should be eager to learn more about Russia. (*Soviet Russia*, pp. 5-6)

But interest in the Soviet Union was not confined to political circles alone. The rejuvenation of the mass of the people who had been kept down in a rigid class society was an event which had a powerful appeal for every humanist, for everyone who felt that civilisation had little meaning if its fruits could not be enjoyed by those who built it.

"There has ever been in history", wrote poet Rabindranath Tagore, in a letter from the Soviet Union to his friends, "a group of unhonoured men. They are always indeed the majority but they bear the world's burden. They have no time to grow to the stature of men… I have often worried about these people and it has seemed as if there was no help. It is necessary for some people to be on top and if that happens, others must be down below… And yet to confess that civilisation can hold its head high solely on the foundation of the enforced degradation and inhumanity of the majority of mankind is a disgraceful reflection…"

> In Russia they are endeavouring to solve this problem at its root. It is not yet time to pronounce the final judgment on its results but what I see with my own eyes is amazing.

In another letter he wrote,

> what I see is astounding, it is so unlike every other country. The difference is basic. Without the least discrimination they are awakening all humanity from tip to toe.

Tagore on Russian Revolution

In Russia at last! Whichever way I look, I am filled with wonder. It is unlike any other country. It is radically different. From top to bottom they are rousing the whole community up without distinction....

It is astonishing to watch the extraordinary vigour with which education spreads throughout Russian society. The measure of education is not merely the number involved, but its thoroughness; its intensity. What abundant preparation, what tremendous efforts, so that no one should remain helpless or idle. Not in European Russia alone, but also among the semi-civilised races of Central Asia, they have opened the flood-gates of education. There is no limit to the effort made to bring the latest fruits of science to them. The theatres here are crowded to over-flowing, but those who come to them are peasants and workers. Nowhere are they humiliated. In the few institutions I have visited so far, I have seen the awakening of their spirit and joy of self-respect....

Again and again, I have asked myself; How has such great miracle been possible? The answer that I have received in my mind is that here there is no barrier of greed... Their astonishingly quick progress has made me happy and jealous at the same time... While in Moscow I particularly liked one characteristic of Soviet administration, and that was the pleasing fact that there was no conflict of interest between the different races and religions; a truly civilised administration impartially served their common interests.

On his eightieth birthday (1941)

Planning Succeeds

The successful carrying out of the Five Year Plans in the USSR, achieved under the leadership of the Central Committee of the Communist Party of the Soviet Union headed by JV Stalin, put an end once and for all to the debate as to whether planning can produce results, as to whether crisis and unemployment are inevitable in the epoch of industrial and technological advance and above all, as to whether Socialism can work. The effect of this victory was worldwide.

Influence on India

In 1936, in his presidential speech before the Lucknow session of the Congress, Nehru drew attention to the sharp contrast between the conditions in the capitalist and socialist world, especially as they had developed since 1929-30.

"Everywhere", he said, "conflicts grew and a great depression overwhelmed the world and there was progressive deterioration everywhere expect in the wide flung territories of the USSR where, in marked contrast with the rest of the world, astonishing progress was made in every direction".

The victory of socialist reconstruction in the USSR gave a powerful impetus to socialist idea all over the world and in our country too. It strengthened the communist and the working class movements and also influenced the advanced sections of the Congress. The writings and speeches of those leaders who laid the foundation of the Congress Socialist Party bear eloquent testimony to this.

Take, for instance, Acharya Narendra Dev's speech as the president of the First Session of the Congress Socialist Party in 1934.

> The fact that the Soviet state advanced rapidly despite the hostility of an antagonistic world and even in the midst of widespread economic crisis is itself proof positive that it has a message to give. It is not necessary that other countries should traverse all the stages Russia has passed through, nor is it necessary that we should implicitly follow the Russian plans in every little detail. The policies can only be adjudged with reference to concrete circumstances of each case but it is also clear that the Russian experiment has undoubtedly much to teach and has facilitated the task of others who may have to embark upon the socialist experiment.

The Indian people have deeply appreciated the unflinching support that the USSR has always given to the cause of India's freedom and the rights of all people to be sovereign and independent.

The friendship that has grown between the peoples of India and USSR is, therefore, not a sudden phenomenon. Its foundation has been laid by the course of the history of our national movement over many years.

Romesh Chandra and World Peace Council

The World Peace Council was founded in 1950 almost simultaneously with the start of the Cold War. It was an international organisation that advocated for peace and had many prominent members including Paul Robeson, Pablo Neruda, Jean-Paul Sartre, W.E.B. Du Bois, Diego Rivera and D.D. Kosambi. Romesh Chandra joined the World Peace Council in 1953 and became the General Secretary in 1966 and its President in 1977. In his own words, "Peace is not just the absence of war. Peace is not just what some people call survival. We are not interested in a survival which means the status quo of hunger and poverty and racism and racial discrimination for hundreds of millions of people. That is not the survival that we want. Peace today is inextricably linked with the struggle for national independence and liberation; peace is linked with the struggle to end racism and racial discrimination". Romesh would always emphasise that the peace movement was a movement against imperialism. Peace meant struggling against the Vietnam war for the Vietnamese, but also it meant struggling against apartheid in South Africa, it meant liberation in Asia and Africa, the struggle against imperialism. It meant and means today the liberation of Palestine. Peace did not mean, as Martin Luther King Jr. said, the absence of tension, but the presence of justice.

That friendship has been further cemented in the period that has passed since, as India, together with many other countries of Asia and Africa, won national freedom.

Today, India, China and the USSR, the three greatest countries of the world, stand together, despite differences in their economic and social systems, in the common struggle for the defence of peace. They have drawn closer to each other. They are forging ties of economic and cultural cooperation with each other and with the resurgent countries of Asia and Africa.

In the USSR, in the People's Republic of China and in the other countries that have broken away from the camp of capitalism, the peoples of the east find their staunchest allies and their most sincere friends. This has been seen in the economic agreements which the USSR has made with several states in Asia and Africa.

This has been seen in the stand the USSR has taken on the issues of Goa and Kashmir, on the issues of Korea, Vietnam and Oman, on the issue of military pacts that threaten peace in Asia and menace the freedom of the Asian and African states.

No More the Law of the Jungle

A vivid demonstration of the role of the USSR in relation to the states of Asia and Africa, took place a year ago when Egypt was subjected to brutal aggression. Today, once again the USSR has issued stern warning against those who menace the freedom of Syria and seek to reimpose colonial slavery on the Arab peoples.

These events show that with the emergence of socialism as a world system and with its increasing strength in the political, economic and military sphere, with the growth of the peace movement, the possibility has opened out for the first time in history, of putting an end to the law of the jungle in the relations between states. This is a law which proclaimed that might was right, a law which permitted powerful countries to impose their will on small and weak countries with impunity. The cause peace finds on its side not only the common man who has always abhorred war and violence but also powerful states able and prepared to bar the path of those who seek world domination through brutal force.

For every patriotic Indian, for every socialist, for every humanist and every lover of peace, the Fortieth Anniversary of the October Revolution is therefore, a memorable event. It is necessary that this event is celebrated in a fitting manner in every part of our country with the widest popular participation.

The Politburo of the Central Committee of the Communist Party of India has therefore given the call for such celebration and it confidently expects that the call will awake response from every patriotic party and every section of our people.

(*New Age Weekly*, November 07, 1957)

Leaders of the Non-Aligned Movement

Jawaharlal Nehru, Prime Minister of India, Kwame Nkrumah, President of Ghana, Gemal Abdel Nasser, President of United Arab Republic, Sukarno, President of Indonesia, Josip Broz Tito, President of Yugoslavia, 1960.

11

November Revolution and Under-Developed Countries

B.T. Ranadive

The forty-third anniversary of the Great November Revolution once more reminds the world, the working class and toiling people of the world, of the great and historic changes since 1917 when the working class of Russia under the leadership of the Bolshevik Party, led by Lenin, established the first socialist state in the world. Subjected to economic blockade, military intervention and every kind of pressure, the first socialist state survived, thanks to its own inner strength, the firm determination of the liberated people never to allow landlords and capitalists to exploit them again, and the warm fraternal support extended to it by the working class of the world, especially of the advanced countries of Europe.

Peace Policy

From its inception, true to its international outlook, the Soviet state, under the leadership of Lenin, proclaimed co-existence among nations belonging to different social systems and took a stand against war. Stalin followed a firm policy of peace despite imperialist provocations.

The Soviet state convinced the world that it did not believe in settling international disputes through war and massacre. Lenin analysed the cause of the war and pointed his accusing finger at the imperialists, who unleashed murderous wars in pursuit of their aims to dominate the world, to redivide it among themselves.

Notwithstanding the firm policy of peace and coexistence pursued by the USSR, the Second World War took place, thanks to imperialist contradictions, the rise of aggressive fascism and the desire of the treacherous imperialist crowd to solve their crisis at the expense of the Soviet land. The Soviet state alone was unable to prevent imperialist conspiracy of war. The strength of the imperialist-capitalist world as yet dominated the world scene.

The end of the Second World War has seen an enormous change in the world balance of forces. The emergence of People's China has altered the balance against imperialism. The people's democracies of Eastern Europe and Asia have further shifted the balance against the imperialists. Now there has emerged a socialist world comprising of 900 million people and 40 per cent of the world territory. The old situation in which only the Soviet Union confronted the rest of the world dominated by imperialism has ended once for all. The military might of the USSR acts as the strong deterrent to imperialist machinations for a new war and brings great strength to the cause of peace.

The increasing economic and political strength of the socialist world has taken away from the imperialists their monopoly of dominating and deciding the world events. This process has been immensely helped and accelerated by the growing collapse of imperialism, the liberation of colonial peoples and full assertion of their will for peace and independence in the world arena. Since the end of the Second World War, more than 1,000 million people have liberated themselves. The governments of many of these countries play an independent role and help the forces of peace and fight attempts to unleash war.

Faced with the invincible might of the national liberation struggles and their resistance to war, in collaboration with the camp of peace and socialism, the forces of aggressive imperialism find themselves checkmated repeatedly. It is not easy for imperialist forces to plunge the world in a new war. The possibilities of nuclear destruction have warned the peoples of all countries against the danger of a war of total destruction and made the task of the imperialists still more difficult. The growing strength of the working class movement in the advanced capitalist countries, the rise of the mass Communist Parties and the strength of the mass peace movement all combine to rebuff imperialist provocations for a new war.

The rapid strides in Communist construction in the Soviet Union under the Seven Year Plan, the great victories in socialist construction in China and European peoples democracies are smashing the imperialist veto on the economic progress of underdeveloped countries. The grand prospect was opened up before the underdeveloped countries to building their economies free from outside domination if only they relied on their own strength and used effectively the disinterested help given by the USSR and the socialist camp. The USSR today is in a position to supply the underdeveloped countries, all that they need for their advance and the latter need no longer be dependent on the imperialists, nor accept the onerous and enslaving political and economic terms which they lay down for their 'aid'.

Economic Leap

The tempestuous growth of the economy of the USSR and countries of the socialist camp is already turning the economic tide in favour of socialism and against imperialism and capitalism. According to the recent estimates, the volume of industrial production of all socialist countries in 1959 exceeded more than five times the pre- Second World War level, while the industrial output of the capitalist countries only doubled. Gross industrial output in the USSR in 1959 was approximately forty times bigger than in 1913. Compared with 1958 the increase in industrial production in the

USSR in 1959 was more than 11 per cent, in the People's Republic of China 39.3 per cent, Poland 8.8 per cent, Czechoslovakia 10.9 per cent, the German Democratic Republic 12 per cent, Hungary 12 per cent, Rumania 11.1 per cent, Bulgaria 25 per cent and the Korean People's Democratic Republic 53 per cent.

People's China will soon beat Great Britain in the production of steel and the Soviet Union, after the completion of its mighty Seven Year Plan, will outdistance the USA in many branches of production.

Under the Seven Year Plan the USSR is creating new records and progressing at a rate unthinkable for capitalist society. Annual targets are being exceeded and surpassed. As the resolution of the plenary meeting of the central committee of the CPSU adopted on 18 July 1960 states:

> The nationwide movement for pre-schedule fulfillment of the Seven Year Plan, the strengthening of the Party organisations' leadership of economic construction, made it possible during the past 18 months to considerably exceed the rates of growth of industrial production and of the development of transport envisaged in the Plan.

The increase in the output of industrial goods amounted to over 11 per cent in 1959, instead of 7.7 per cent targeted under the Plan, and during the first six months of the current year the growth was more than 10 per cent, as against 8.1 per cent, envisaged in the annual plan. Heavy industry, the basis of the national economy, is developing at a rapid pace.

The full significance of these facts can be understood from the fact that the Seven Year Plan of national economic development of the Soviet Union envisages increase in industrial production by 80 per cent, and the production of means of production by 85-88 per cent; the production of electric power will more than double, and the volume of chemical production will approximately treble. It is these targets that are being fulfilled ahead of schedule and are likely to be surpassed at the end of the Seven Year Plan for 1959-65.

Two Lines

But for this developing economic strength of the USSR, and the socialist camp, the outlook for the underdeveloped countries would have been black indeed. For, the law of the development of capitalist system necessarily divides the capitalist countries into advanced and backward countries. Capitalist development not only leads to polarisation of wealth and poverty within individual countries, but also concentrates scientific and industrial advance and immense richness in a few countries, while condemning the rest to backward technique and poverty – to play the role of hewers of wood and drawers of water – of suppliers of raw materials to the advanced countries.

Lenin had long ago pointed out that capitalism divides the nations into a small number of oppressing, powerful, privileged imperialist nations enjoying full rights and the overwhelming majority of oppressed, dependent and semi-dependent nations. One has only to contrast the concentration of wealth in a handful of western imperialist countries – USA, Britain, France – with the degradation and destitution found in backward countries to understand how capitalism has divided the world into haves and have not nations. The imperialist-capitalist system can maintain itself only by perpetuating this inequality. The advanced capitalist nations can never agree to give up their privileged position which enables them to exploit the backward peoples. They, therefore, work desperately to perpetuate this state of affairs notwithstanding their glib talk of 'aid' and 'help' to the underdeveloped countries to build their economies. The outlook and prospects of newly liberated countries of Asia and Africa would have been dismal indeed if the initiative for 'help' and 'aid' had remained in the hands of these few privileged imperialist countries of the west.

The Soviet Union has an entirely different approach to the question of the development of the underdeveloped countries. The socialist system believes in and bases itself on economic equality among nations and peoples, on the widespread diffusion of well-being, prosperity and scientific advance among all peoples. In rendering disinterested aid to the underdeveloped countries the Soviet state is following the policy laid down by Lenin who even before the October Revolution stated: 'we shall exert every effort in order to come closer and merge with the Mongols, Persians, Indians, Egyptians' and that 'we shall do our best to render those people who are more backward and oppressed than we are, disinterested cultural aid'.

Khrushchev Speaks

At a meeting of Bhilai metallurgical workers in February 1960, Khrushchev described Soviet policy as follows:

> We consider it our international duty to help the nations that have thrown off the political power of the colonialists to free themselves completely from all the fetters of dependence, put an end to economic backwardness and achieve social progress and prosperity. Our economic and technical cooperation with the countries of Asia and Africa is the logical continuation of the fraternal support we have invariably and consistently given to the anti-imperialist liberation movement of the oppressed peoples.

Contrasting Soviet policy with the policy of the western imperialist countries, Khrushchev said:

> It is the desire of the Soviet Union and other socialist states that our economic and technical cooperation with these countries should accelerate the development of the former colonies and semi-colonies, and strengthen their national independence. But there are some people in the west who use their 'aid' as the instrument of a new colonial policy, as a means of safeguarding the interest of monopoly capital and deepening the political division of the world into hostile groupings... And so those who retarded and would still like to retard the economic development of India and of other countries that have liberated themselves from colonial domination will be put to shame.
>
> They are speculating on rendering these countries economic 'aid' in the form of consumer goods. But these goods are soon used up and the recipient of such 'aid' is obliged to apply again and again for more goods to those who produce them, to those who, under the guise of assistance, are reaping huge profits while keeping the people of the

> economically underdeveloped countries in a state of dependence. We prefer to render genuine assistance so that every country that has thrown off colonial domination might be able in a short space of time to build up its economy and produce the commodities it needs.

The economic developments of the last ten years more sharply bring into contrast the two processes in underdeveloped countries. They show that but for the economic strength of the Soviet Union and the socialist camp, and its will to render disinterested aid, these countries would have found themselves completely at the mercy of the privileged imperialist nations. These newly liberated countries even now to a large extent are dependent for their exports and imports on the western markets of imperialist countries. Though their trade and economic relations with the Soviet Union and the socialist camp are growing, still they are to a great extent dominated by their economic ties with western countries.

Thanks to this, they are subject to unequal exchange, to the blast of capitalist recession and their capacity to import machinery for their industrial advance is being constantly impaired by the

Economic Planning in India

After independence, the legacy of the anti-colonial struggle made economic planning a very important part of newly independent India. The second five year plan was called the Mahalanobis plan, and was influenced by both Nehru's ideas and Soviet planning. The primary purpose of the programme was to raise the level of income and also to achieve economic autonomy. As described in the article, "development of heavy industry" was an extremely important part of the second five year plan and was directly influenced by the Soviet planning style. However, Nehru was well aware that a country like India would always require the need to balance agriculture and industry. Therefore, even while emphasising the development of infrastructure and heavy industry, the Indian plans had to give due importance to the question of land and agricultural development.

depreciation of their exports. All this is forcing them to resort to credits and loans from the west on onerous and sometimes compromising terms which is likely to jeopardise their future. In this background, the aid received by them from the Soviet Union and other socialist countries has been the only influence which has counteracted the evil effects of their unequal ties with the west.

Dependence on Imperialism

The annual reports of the UNO on underdeveloped countries fully bear out these conclusions.

These countries in the first place are plagued by antiquated feudal and semi-feudal land relations which their new rulers have not liquidated with the result that the productive forces in agriculture are not able to have a free play. With the backward technique of agriculture which this imposes on them, they are unable to meet the rising demand for food of their own peoples. The underdeveloped countries also could not meet the raw material demand of the west with whom they were hitherto economically tied and from whom they have to get essential capital goods for their own advance. These countries are, therefore, too much dependent on their foreign trade with the western countries for their advance.

Facts regarding ECAFE[1] (The Economic Commission for Asia and the Far East) countries, given in the UN Economic Survey 1959 give revealing evidence as regards the results of this excessive dependence on foreign trade with capitalist countries of the west and the prospects they hold out to these countries. Reviewing the developments of the last three decades the survey concludes:

> It seems clear, then, that the region cannot place too much reliance on increasing exports of primary products to the industrial countries... On any reasonable assumption as to the desirable rate of growth of their national product, it appears, therefore, that hardly any country of the region can look forward to an economic development in which the

1 ECAFE was established by United Nations in 1947.

> growth of exports of primary products to the industrial countries plays the leading role. (p. 96)

Thanks to the backwardness of the countries and the unequal exchange imposed on them by the imperialist countries, during the last three decades, between 1928-1957 imports have increased more rapidly than exports. The former have increased by 63 per cent while the latter have increased by only 22 per cent. By the thirties, the export surplus of these areas had already changed into an import surplus.

Price of Dependence

Not only did the region – primary exporting countries of the ECAFE – see its export surplus change into an import surplus, it also became a cereals importing region whereas it was formerly a cereals exporting region:

> The decline in per capita foodgrain production in the Burma-India-Pakistan area, with over two-thirds of the total foodgrain production of the ECAFE primary exporting countries, accounted for the change in the position of the group from a net exporter to a net importer of cereals. Gross imports of foodgrains constitute a larger proportion of total imports in 1955-57 than in 1928, despite the attempt by several countries to grow more grain to reduce imports, even at the cost of reducing exports of other primary products, such as sugar, cotton and jute.
>
> The per capita annual consumption of cereals fell in India, from 163 kilogram in 1934-38 to 152 kilograms in 1955-57, the decline in Pakistan for the corresponding period was from 176 to 168 kilograms. Ceylon and Singapore also showed declines, though other countries of the region showed increases. Thus by far the largest part of the population of this area suffered a decline in per capita cereals consumption. Though the report says that the decline in India is probably exaggerated, yet it admits that there is a decline.

The failure of these countries to produce their own food requirements has increased their dependence on western countries and acted as a brake on the advance they could have registered otherwise.

> Despite the progress made, the critical need to import staple foods has forced the ECAFE primary exporting countries to divert a not negligible proportion of their foreign exchange earnings from capital goods imports necessary for economic development. Between 1927-29 and 1955-57, their net balance on cereals changed from $128 million net earnings to a net expenditure of $237 million in terms of 1955-57 purchasing power over manufactured goods. In a way, this adverse situation has deprived the area of one-fourth of the increase in its total earnings that it secured in this period of about three decades.

Failure to liquidate antiquated land relations together with the unequal exchange imposed by the industrial countries of the west has produced this calamitous situation.

For these countries, the main source of their earning their way to industrialisation is exports. But the crisis ridden economies of western countries create tremendous instability in the volume and value of exports and make the economies of these countries insecure. The exploitation inherent in the trade of underdeveloped countries with the imperialist countries enhance the instability and insecurity.

Adverse Trend

Over three decades the external purchasing power of exports of the ECAFE primary exporting countries has grown less than their production. On the other hand, the rate of which the imports of the ECAFE primary exporting countries increased between 1928 and 1955-57 was almost than three times of the purchasing power of the exports. This has altered the trade balance of the ECAFE countries from an aggregate export surplus in 1928 of over one billion dollars worth of manufactured goods at 1955-57 prices to an annual import surplus of somewhat less than a hundred million dollars during 1955-57 at current prices. The primary exporting countries of the region had a net import surplus of a little over $750 million during 1955-57.

The slow growth of exports is partly due to the competition from advanced industrial countries themselves:

> The gains made by the industrial countries, particularly in North America in the production of primary commodities, have had opposite effects on world trade. On the one hand, as noted above, they have reduced the import demand of the United States for primary productions; on the other, the United States has increased its share in the export of cereals to other industrial countries, and to the primary producing countries themselves.
>
> The share of the primary producing countries in primary exports has thus declined in two directions; they have lost ground to the United States in their exports to Western Europe (and Japan) and in their exports to each other. Accordingly, they have become more dependent on the industrial countries than in the 'twenties for imports of food for their population and of raw materials for their industries.

The volume of exports of seventeen commodities which in 1927-29 accounted for 82 per cent of the total value of the primary exports from eleven ECAFE countries increased by a little over one-fifth during the three decades since 1928. Even so the volume of exports is dominated by only two commodities, namely, petroleum and rubber. Excluding petroleum, it remained about the same as in 1927-29; excluding petroleum and rubber, it declined by about a quarter. The decline is widely spread over many traditional exports of the region, such as rice, tin, cotton, jute, sugar, oils and oilseeds (other than copra), tobacco, hides and skins, spices, wool and coffee. While the volume of many commodities has declined in this region, the exports of these commodities from Africa and Latin America have increased.

If the total volume of exports increased by 20 per cent, the real unit value of primary exports increased by only 7 per cent and the purchasing power by 29 per cent. For the group of eleven ECAFE countries, the value of net exports measured in terms of manufactured goods at 1957-58 prices increased between 1927-28 and 1955-57 by a little less than a billion dollars or by 22 per cent of the total net exports during 1927-29. Petroleum contributed substantially to these earnings, accounting for more than 80 per cent of the total increase from primary exports. Excluding petroleum, the purchasing power of the primary exports of ECAFE area increased by only 3 per cent of the 1927-29 exports of primary products (other than petroleum).

Thus, the total gains secured by the ECAFE countries from primary exports have been small. Moreover, they are concentrated in only three commodities, namely, petroleum, rubber and tea, together accounting for more than half the earnings in 1955-57. The first two have raised their share from a little over one-fifth in 1927-29 to two-fifths in 1955-57.

These gains besides, have been geographically concentrated in a few small countries. Between 1927-29 and 1955-57 the Burma-India- Pakistan sub-continent (India as it was then) and Indonesia, with together seven-eighth of the population of the eleven countries, lost between them a primary export capacity of over $400 million while the smaller countries have gained by as much as $1.2 billion. The gains are mainly due to petroleum, rubber and tea.

Moreover, it must be remembered that the production of the three commodities which have gained in value is mostly in foreign hands. As a result, even though the gains accrued statistically to the geographical area of the ECAFE primary exporting countries, a sizable portion was not available to them to finance their imports. As the survey points out, the Iranian oil consortium withdrew from its share of profit, an amount averaging $140 million a year during the three years ending on 20 March 1958. Similarly, account must be taken of transfer of profits abroad from other countries of the region. As a result the gain in the export based capacity to import is substantially lower than the figure arrived at on the basis of f.o.b. (Freight on Board) value of exports.

> The problems of long-term sluggishness of growth in the purchasing power of exports of the ECAFE primary countries have been compounded by violent short-term fluctuations in export earnings – the fluctuation in total earnings magnify the repercussions on the capital import programmes for economic development. The sharp decline in capital goods imports in 1958 in several countries, following a slump in export proceeds, reveals the effects of such disturbances.

In the post-war period from 1948 to 1958, the average annual fluctuations in the export earnings of the ECAFE primary exporting countries were of the order of 14 per cent. The volume of exports fluctuated, on the average, by 9 per cent and unit value by 12 per cent.

Impact of Crisis

The crisis ridden economies of industrial countries are in the main responsible for these violent fluctuations.

> The major reasons for short-term instability in primary markets, on the demand side are the cyclical fluctuations in the income and output of the industrial countries. During the post-war period, there were cyclical downswings in the United States on three occasions in 1949, 1954, 1958... in 1958 when the decline in United States demand was associated with the faltering of industrial production in Japan and western Europe, there was a sharp decline in the export earnings of ECAFE primary exporting countries.
>
> Though the total volume of net imports of primary commodities into the industrial areas was barely affected, the sensitivity of commodity markets to the changing economic climate in the major buying countries was sufficient to reduce prices and export earnings of the under-developed countries by 7 to 8 per cent from mid-1957 to mid-1958. This drop, reinforced by a continuing albeit slight rise in the import prices of manufactured goods in the face of the industrial recession, represents a loss in import capacity equivalent to about six years lending to the under-developed countries by the International Bank for Reconstruction and Development (IBRD) at 1956-57 rates. (*U.N. World Economic Survey*, 1958)

What chance has genuine industralisation under these circumstances?

While world exports of manufactured goods doubled during the last three decades, the exports of manufactures of ECAFE countries increased by only 10 per cent. Except India, no country has really embarked upon the production of capital or similar goods, building materials being an exception. The emphasis has been on producing consumer goods. Textiles have been the favourite but other industries include sugar refining, edible oils, aerated waters and alcoholic beverages, tobacco products, footwear and leather goods, domestic utensils.

This result is fully in conformity with the designs and policy of the western nations who seek to exploit these countries and perpetuate their backwardness.

In the post-1958 recession year things improved a little but could not make any fundamental change for the ECAFE regions. Good harvests, industrial boom in Japan and industrial advance in India placed the region in a better position. In the under-developed countries as a whole, exports recovered more rapidly than in industrial countries. But for the primary exporting countries of the ECAFE region exports declined by 13 per cent between the first half-years of 1957 and 1958; between the second half years of 1957 and 1958, the decline was 6 per cent.

In the first quarter of 1959 the exports of the ECAFE primary producing countries registered a further decline of some 4 per cent as compared to the first quarter of 1958. The terms of trade have improved since 1958. Export price of primary products increased by 4.6 per cent while on the import side world prices of manufactures decreased slightly (by 2 per cent in the first half of 1959).

Way of Financing

How then have these countries – the ECAFE primary exporting countries – managed to finance their import surplus, since exports could not pay for them? How were they able to get vital capital goods for themselves and the maintenance need of their economies?

Firstly, because temporarily the foreign debt interest burden was lightened during the course of the war; secondly, by running down the foreign exchange reserves they had accumulated during the war; and thirdly, by running new debts and inducing further foreign private investments. The foreign interest and debt repayment burden was considerably lightened by the inflation of primary commodity prices during the war and in the early post-war years and by the wartime accumulation of foreign exchange reserves which enabled many countries to repay their foreign debts.

There was, thus, a net reduction in the rates of interest and dividend payments to export earnings in a number of countries. The ratio for India declined from 10 per cent in 1928-29 to some 4 per cent in 1955-57 largely owing to debt retirement. It is now likely to exceed the 1928 ratio, thanks to fresh debts. The ratio for Indonesia declined from 23 to 10 per cent over the same period.

While the small addition made by private capital imports in the late twenties to the region's export based capacity to import declined in the 1950s, a new item, donations and official loans, made its appearance in post-war balance of payments, as a compensatory item. The ratio of foreign aid and capital inflow to exports during 1955-57 was considerably larger than in 1928. This inflow into ten countries of the ECAFE region amounted to an annual average of 1.1 billion dollars during the three years from 1955 to 1957, or a quarter of the purchasing power derived from merchandise exports alone.

Foreign Debt

There is a steep rise in India's foreign debt, private and official. During the course of her two five year plans, India had to rely heavily on foreign borrowing and the result is seen in the following figures. India's foreign private debt was ₹255.8 crore in June 1948. Between 1955 and 1959, according to the Reserve Bank Bulletin of April 1960 the debt increased as follows:

Foreign Debt (in crores of Rupees)

Year		1955	1957	1958	1959
Private	Non-Banking	456	542	571	593
	Banking	57	48	52	59
Official		201	463	668	926
Total		714	1053	1291	1578

Within four years the foreign debt had increased 100 per cent. The World Bank Mission which visited India in 1958, estimated on the basis of loans made prior to the Second Plan that India would have to earmark 8 per cent of total external receipts on current account to repay her interest and debt charges at the peak period in 1960-64. The World Bank Mission declared that India had already mortgaged her future foreign exchange resources and for the Third Plan India seeks to have foreign credits worth ₹2,600 crore.

Of course, some of these loans come from socialist countries for vital Indian projects and they are free from all elements of exploitation. They promote the country's development. The rest come from western countries. The total authorised aid from the USA, United Kingdom, West Germany, Japan and IBRD till 30 November 1959 amounts to ₹1,071 crore. The total aid authorised till 30 November 1959 from the USSR alone amounts to ₹322 crore.

Effect of 'Aid'

What has been the result, of this 'aid' for the primary exporting countries of the ECAFE region (the same verdict may not apply fully to each country but by and large is true of all):

> While the establishment of these industries (new industries) has reduced their dependence on the industrial countries for the relatively simple manufactures such as textile products, the primary export countries are almost completely dependent upon industrial countries for their increasing need of capital goods imports to sustain their development programmes. It is this dependence which makes the gap between the purchasing power of the exports of these primary exporting countries and their import needs more disturbing. They have remained more vulnerable than the industrial countries since their economic growth is more critically dependent on their capacity to import than is the case with the industrial countries. Indeed, for several of them, even their present levels of living hang precariously on the prospects encountered by not more than two or three commodities in the world market.

This is so because the western countries with all their 'aid' and trade do nothing to set these economies on their own feet, make them self- reliant. And this is precisely where the USSR came in and introduced new features in aid and trade which immensely helped the underdeveloped countries.

In the first place, it must be realised that the primary exporting countries of the world conduct their trade overwhelmingly with the capitalist countries, though their trade with the USSR and the socialist camp is increasing. Thus, for instance in 1957 these countries exported $2,650 million worth of beverages, food and tobacco to North America, $4,450 million worth to Western Europe and $230 million to centrally planned economies. The corresponding figures for crude materials are $1,520 million, $4,700 million and $708 million and for manufactures and semi-manufactures $923 million, $1,551 million and $269 million.

Socialist Help

Even then the extremely beneficial effects of the agreements reached by these countries with the socialist countries is already in evidence:

> During recent years, the centrally planned economies entered into a number of bilateral agreements with several primary producing countries which resulted in a significant increase in their exports of primary commodities. At a time when world markets were depressed, such agreements providing for an exchange of a stipulated amount of goods at fixed prices had a stabilizing effect on the foreign trade proceeds of the exporters of primary commodities. An important advantage of such agreements was that they enabled these countries to exchange surplus commodities for capital goods.(*U.N. World Economic Survey,* 1958, p. 165)

The effect of these policies can be seen from the following. The large purchases of Egyptian cotton in 1955 and 1956, which took place during the period of falling world prices, reduced considerably the pressure of existing supply on prices and its effect on Egyptian economy. The share of the centrally planned economies in Egyptian cotton exports rose from 14 per cent in 1954 to 27 per cent in 1955, 34 per cent in 1956 and about 46 per cent in 1957.

Similarly, the bilateral clearing agreements signed with centrally planned economies in 1954, providing for the exchange of Burmese rice for capital goods and other manufactures enabled Burma to dispose of its large surplus at relatively stable prices.

The five-year bilateral agreement signed in 1952 by Ceylon and People's China enabled Ceylon to dispose of a large proportion of its rubber at annually fixed prices, at a time when world prices were falling sharply. The effect of this transaction on the economy of Ceylon was considerably strengthened by the fact that, in return People's China offered substantial amounts of rice at prices more favourable than those prevailing in the tightening world markets. In 1957, a new five year agreement was signed, providing for an annual exchange of 2,00,000 tons of rice for 30,000 tons of rubber at prices prevailing at the time of signing the contract, thus stabilising rice and rubber prices in the trade between the two countries (*World Economic Survey,* p. 166).

In 1959 alone, the USSR and eastern European countries signed 25 new agreements with the ECAFE countries excluding People's China, North Vietnam and North Korea. Of these 25 agreements, two were treaties of commerce, four were long-term trade agreements, seven were short- term trade agreements and seven were credit agreements. Besides these People's China entered into a number of agreements with the countries of this region.

The 1959 agreement between Indonesia and the USSR provides that the USSR would supply to Indonesia machineries, equipment, materials and technical assistance for the construction of two iron and steel plants, one superphosphate factory, 650 kilometres of highway, two mechanised rice farming units under a USSR credit of $100 million. Another agreement operative through 1960 provides that Indonesia would supply rubber, hides and coffee – its primary products to USSR while the latter agrees to supply machinery, equipment, fertilisers, paper, etc. Thus; at one stroke the problem of export surplus of primary products and import of essential means of production is being solved. Indonesia has similarly traded its raw materials for machinery, etc., with Bulgaria, while it has secured under another agreement credit from Czechoslovakia for constructing a cement plant and 34 power stations.

Perhaps, the most outstanding of these agreements is between India and the USSR under which the latter grants a credit of roubles 1,500 million (₹180 crore) to India at 2.5 per cent interest for helping India implement her Third Five Year Plan and expanding trade between the two countries. Repayment of this credit and also previous ones, can be made in rupees instead of sterling which will be utilised by the USSR for purchase of Indian tea, shoes, hides and skins and other primary products. Thus, once more the problem of disposing primary products and securing vital capital goods is being solved and a country is being helped along the lines of self-sustained growth.

India has signed agreements with Poland, Romania, Czechoslovakia, trading her primary products for capital equipment, etc.

New Relations

Obviously these agreements play a tremendous role in foiling the imperialist game to subjugate the economies of under-developed countries, to overwhelm them. By taking away surplus primary products and exchanging them for machinery and means of production, they open the way to these economies to independent and self-sustained growth – the only condition being that these countries put their own house in order and are prepared to end their one-sided economic dealings with the west. Thanks to these new economic relations, the newly liberated countries are able to break the blockade organised by their former rulers against them. Thus in 1958, when the Dutch cancelled shipping services to Indonesia to create difficulties for her, the Soviet Union came to Indonesia's rescue by selling her twelve ships on advantageous terms.

The newly liberated countries, wanting to maintain their political and economic independence, could not miss the significance of the new trade relations, could not but see the difference between their two trading partners. The exchange and trade between the underdeveloped countries, between the countries of the ECAFE region and the USSR could not but develop under these circumstances, though it must be said that it could have and should have developed much more rapidly had it not been for the dual role of the ruling classes in these countries.

It is, therefore, but proper that trade between the under-developed countries and the USSR should increase. Trade between the centrally planned economies and the primary exporting countries was at a higher level in 1959 than in 1958. The principal increase was in shipments to the Soviet Union which had declined slightly between 1957 and 1958. It has been computed that the volume of trade of seven countries – India, Indonesia, Ceylon, Pakistan, Burma, the Malayan Federation and Cambodia, increased seven times between 1955 and 1958.

But it is not only through mutually beneficial trade relations which stabilise their economies and give them capital goods in exchange that the USSR is helping the underdeveloped countries to stand on their feet. The USSR gives direct aid to build new industries to lay the basis for industrialisation and thus enables these countries to rear independent economies free from outside interference. The USSR extends huge credits to these countries at nominal rates of interest and besides gives technical guidance and know-how to build new heavy industry – the foundation of free self-sustained economy. No other country has done so much to help these newly liberated countries as the USSR.

The Soviet Union has granted about £890 million (₹1,200 crore) in loans to underdeveloped countries, according to Mikhail Malakhov, Vice-Chairman of the Council of Ministers, State Committee for External Relations. About 300 industrial establishments will be built in these countries with Soviet assistance.

Industrial Growth

The most remarkable feature is that these credits are given precisely to build heavy industry and accelerate the process of industrialisation of these countries.

The agreement signed between the USSR and Indonesia in February 1960 stipulates the cooperation of the Soviet government with the government of Indonesia in building industrial and other credits, including enterprises of iron and steel, non-ferrous metals and chemical industries, in using atomic energy for peaceful purposes and in building textile mills and agricultural units required for the general economic development of the Republic of Indonesia. Soviet agencies will render assistance in the training of Indonesian experts for work. The repayment of the credit and the payment of interest on it shall be effected by Indonesian government through deliveries of Indonesian goods to the Soviet Union and or in pounds sterling, as well as in other freely convertible currencies. Along with this it was agreed that there should be a long-term trade agreement which will deal with the purchase by the Soviet Union of greater quantities than hitherto of Indonesian rubber and other items of traditional Indonesian export, as well as the delivery by the Soviet Union of commodities in which Indonesia is interested.

These agreements and credits thus serve a double purpose. They supply these countries with means of production for industrialisation and accept in payment the raw materials and products which are surplus.

With Soviet assistance, Ceylon also will build a plant producing 35,000 tons of rolled steel per year. This will be very important in Ceylon's economic advance. No wonder large sections of Ceylonese people see in this the dawn of a new industrial era.

By 1958 Afghanistan had secured 480 million roubles worth of such credits; the UAR 1,100 million roubles worth and Indonesia 400 million roubles worth.

But the most outstanding and striking instance of disinterested aid to an under-developed country is the Soviet credit and help to India for her Second and Third Five Year Plans. India has received considerable 'aid' from the United States of America at exorbitant rates of interest. In fact American credits are bigger than credits received from the Soviet Union. Yet there is a vital difference between the two, apart from onerous American terms, as regards their effect on national advance. An American publication correctly states:

> In the case of India, about 80 per cent of the United States grants was used for the purchase of industrial commodities, and about 55 per cent of the total purchase consisted of machinery products. But of the latter, the largest proportion consisted of railroad equipment and motor vehicles and engines, much less of industrial machinery to be installed in factories. Soviet credits to India, on the other hand, are to be used primarily for the construction of such projects as the steel mill, petroleum extraction and refining installations, fertiliser plants, etc.(pp. 63-64, *Soviet Economic Aid*, Joseph Berliner – Council of Foreign Relations, New York).

The Soviet credits are meant for a rapid industrial build-up while American credits are mainly meant to perpetuate India's dependence on the west.

Indo-Soviet Cooperation

What chance had India of advancing her economic development by means of securing surplus from trade with the western countries with the help of credit and technical help given by them? None. India's planners had decided for a new steel plant under the First Plan itself. But unfortunately they relied only on the western countries to help them. The British and American monopolists had no intention of helping them and the First Five Year Plan went without a steel plant.

It was only when the negotiations started with the USSR that the British and German monopolists agreed to offer a plant each. The Bhilai steel plant – the most up-to-date plant built by the Soviet engineers for India is not only a symbol of Indo-Soviet friendship, it is also a monument to the fact that the Soviet Union broke the imperialist blockade and veto on India's progress and cleared the way for further advance.

The Bhilai agreement not only gives India a steel plant but it transfers the know-how and trains Indian engineers to erect plants without help from outside. India's future plants will be entirely erected by Indian engineers who have mastered the know-how in Moscow and Bhilai.

India's Second Five Year Plan placed more emphasis on heavy industry than the first. Here again it was the Soviet Union that underwrote some of the most important and vital projects of the plan. The imperialist did their best to sabotage these projects.

On 9th November 1957, the Soviet government concluded an agreement to give India credit of 500 million roubles (about Rs. 59.53 crore) at 2.5 per cent interest rate for the establishment of the following enterprises in India:

a) A heavy machine building plant with a capacity, at the first stage, for manufacturing 45,000 tons of machinery items per annum;
b) A coal-mining machinery plant with a capacity of 30,000 tons of machinery items per annum;
c) An optical and ophthalmic glass factory;
d) A thermal power station in Neyveli based on lignite with a capacity of 250,000 Kw;
e) Enterprises in the Korba coal fields for mining and treating 2.5 million tons of coal per annum, dressing plant and central mechanical repair shop.

Some of these projects are vitally important for India's advance. They play an important role in smashing imperialist veto on India's progress. The heavy machine building plant is almost the only plant of its kind being built under the Second Plan, the only other comparable plant being the Bhopal Heavy Electricals. For India, which is dependent on the West for machinery, the strategic importance of heavy machine building plant is obvious.

The coal-mining machinery has similar importance and the development of Korba fields has a special significance. Coal mining is done both in public and private sectors in India. The former is lagging behind in production and it is of utmost importance that the lag is overcome through development of Korba fields. Besides nearly 12.5 crore of rupees worth of British capital is invested in the coal industry in the private sector. To break its grip it is necessary to develop the public sector. By giving help to develop the Korba fields, the Soviet Union helps India to have a firm grip over its coal industry.

One of the most important agreements is the agreement to establish an oil refinery in the public sector at Barauni. This will be the first Indian owned oil refinery in India (It started functioning in 1964). Extraction and refining of oil have been in the hands of foreign monopolists in India. As late as 1953, the Government of India entered into agreements with American and British oil companies to build new refineries and made many anti-national commitments and the western monopolists sabotaged any attempt by the public sector to enter in this field.

Now that the government wanted at least one oil refinery in the public sector, the monopolists resisted this attempt and refused to help the government. The World Bank denounced the projects for refineries in the public sector and advised the government to turn them over to the private sector, which meant to foreign monopoly capital. Had it not been for the friendly help from the USSR and Romania, the government of India would have been forced to give up its projects, and surrender before the foreign monopolists. The government neither possessed the know-how nor the necessary means of production. It is precisely these that have been put at its disposal by the USSR and Romania and the new refineries are being built with socialist help. Once more the imperialist veto on India's progress is being smashed with Soviet help. Today in the public sector prospecting of oil and building of new refineries is being done with Soviet and Romanian help.

Third Plan

Finally, there is the big credit for India's Third Plan which underwrites almost all the important projects under the Plan. A ₹180 crore agreement was signed early this year during the visit of N.S.

Khrushchev to India. It provides that the credit will be utilised in the Third Five Year Plan for the following projects:

a) Expansion of the Bhilai Steel Works and its ancillary facilities to increase its capacity to 2.5 million tons of steel a year.
b) Expansion of the heavy machinery plant at Ranchi (Bihar) to its designed capacity of 80,000 tons a year.
c) Expansion and diversification of machinery plant for mining.
d) Completion of the oil refinery at Barauni.
e) Manufacture of heavy electrical equipment.
f) Exploration, development and production of oil and gas by Oil and Natural Gas Corporation at Cambay and in other areas.

A glance at Annexure I to the Third Five Year Plan outline shows that the most vital projects dealing with industry and minerals in the public sector for which foreign exchange is already assured are those covered by agreements with the Soviet Union. There are several other important and vital projects contemplated like the expansion of other steel plants, etc. but for these there is no assurance from the western countries regarding the foreign exchange resources. It appears therefore, that only projects covered by agreements between the USSR and India will be definitely completed; the rest may have to be pruned down due to the opposition of the vested interests from western imperialist countries.

By helping to complete the vital projects under the Second Plan and expand them under the Third Plan and by helping to build new heavy industries, the USSR is playing a great role in India's industrialisation. There is no doubt that the completion of these projects will immensely strengthen India's industrial potential, strengthen the independence of her economy and open the way for further advance. Had it not been for these projects India's industrial advance would have been tremendously slowed down. Even now, because of her reliance on the West, the Second Plan had to be pruned down. Very little would have remained of the Second Plan and still less of the Third Plan had the Soviet Union not come forward with disinterested aid to build India's heavy industry.

No other country has received such timely and generous aid and given such wide opportunities to transform her economy. Of course, India can reap the full benefits of this help if she sets her own house in order, liquidates the antiquated land relations, organises agriculture on cooperative lines and growingly curbs private profiteering. The full benefit of such help can be reaped very rapidly if the country decides to take decisive steps towards socialism. China has shown what can be achieved if this is done. India's ruling class, of course, does not believe in socialism and is, therefore, unable to utilise fully the Soviet aid for releasing the productive forces. That is a matter for Indians to decide. The disinterested Soviet aid in the meanwhile places in the hands of the Indian people all the wherewithal for their economic advance and industrialisation.

Lenin's Behest

Such is the new role of the Soviet Union and the socialist camp led by it in the battle of smaller and weaker nations for equality, economic freedom and advance. Those who struck at the world capitalist system by organising the glorious November Revolution in 1917 are now fulfilling the behest of the great Lenin to aid the weaker nations and countries in economic advance and progress. In the earlier period, they encouraged these people in their fight for political independence and helped them directly or indirectly. While continuing this help to those who are still enslaved, the inheritors of the November Revolution are smashing that barrier between nations – the barrier of inequality and backwardness, which is the last hope of imperialism.

The great economic advance of the socialist camp, the mighty Communist construction that is taking place in the USSR, has thus a tremendous world significance. It is a great source of strength to the underdeveloped countries, a great liberating world force that opens new prospects before underdeveloped peoples and nations. It announces the superiority of the world socialist system over the capitalist system and shows that in the competition between the two, the latter, which cannot exist without enforcing backwardness on nations, is bound to lose.

The entire progressive world hails Soviet achievements in communist construction. The working class of the world, the peaceful nations and peoples of all countries, hail the great Soviet initiative for peace and disarmament, for avoiding nuclear war. They all endorse Khrushchev's appeal to end colonialism once and for all so that peace, freedom and equality among nations are permanently ensured. The Soviet initiative in unmasking U.S. imperialism at the recent UNO Session and the historic part played by Khrushchev will immensely strengthen the struggle for freedom and equality among nations.

The mighty economic advance of the Soviet Union and its initiative to help the underdeveloped countries has strengthened and consolidated the bonds of friendship and solidarity between the people of the Soviet Union and people of Asia and Africa. In the years to come, they will grow still stronger to the discomfiture of the imperialists.

On the occasion of the anniversary of the November Revolution, we greet the glorious Communist Party of the Soviet Union, the government and the people of the Soviet Union. We wish them further successes in the consolidation of peace and Communist construction.

(*New Age Monthly*, November 1960)

The Feldman-Mahalanobis Model

The Feldman-Mahalanobis Model is a model of economic development created independently by Soviet Economist Grigory Feldman in 1928 and Indian Statistician P. C. Mahalanobis in 1953. The essence of the model is a shift in the pattern of industrial investment towards production of capital goods. The strategy suggests that in order to reach a high standard in consumption, it is necessary to first build a high enough capacity in capital goods sector. The model was created as an analytical framework for India's Second Five Year Plan from 1956 to 1961.

During the Second Five Year Plan, rapid industrialisation took place with heavy investment in the Public Sector. Hydro-electric Power Projects and five steel plants were set up. Coal production was increased and new Railway lines were laid down. Tata Institute of Fundamental Research (TIFR) and Atomic Energy Commission were established as research institutions during the Plan.

12

Great October brought Cultural Renaissance

Rajeev Saxena

The Great October Revolution was the single major factor that changed the literary scene decisively in the world. It struck a new note of hope in the rhapsody of Indian cultural renaissance that had vibrated to dispel gloom under the harsh colonial British rule.

Tagore called the Great October a "dawn of a new age" and Munshi Premchand as "the Sun of a new civilisation". The great fiction writer and one of the founders of the progressive writers movement, Munshi Premchand, said:

> ...now the sun of a new civilisation is rising from the west which has uprooted this atrocious capitalism... All glory to this civilisation which is putting an end to the rich and the institution of private property and sooner or later the entire world would surely follow it.
>
> That the civilisation is incompatible to social structure or religious ethos or environment of any particular country (evidently he was rebutting the argument of Indian conservatives and imperialist hostile propagandists – RS), would be a thoroughly unfounded logic...

Dispelling Gloom

The early anti-imperialist Hindi writers in the latter half of nineteenth century, led by Bharatendu Harishchandra attempted to dispel the gloom of the post-1857 revolt period by ridiculing the British ruling circles and by depicting the stark reality of hunger, famines and burden of heavy taxes.

The tool to generate a new renaissance was revivalism, the song of the glory of this ancient country, the spirit of proving that the people of India were nothing inferior, in fact superior, to the British usurpers. It laid down the basis of critical realism and its humanitarian approach.

This trend was further developed by the next generation of poets like Maithili Sharan Gupta and other writers led by the towering personality of that generation, Mahavir Prasad Dwivedi. In Dwivedi and his other contemporaries, we already find echoes of the socialist ideas that penetrated in India through the British left movement.

The British imperialists and the information media controlled by them, further tightened the cordon sanitaire after the Great October in order to keep their Indian colony free of socialist 'infection'. The anti-socialist disinformation campaign that they launched against it, however, generated a sympathetic note in Indian hearts and reading between the lines, the Indian nationalist press countered and rebuffed it.

The fragrance of revolution could not in this way be kept out of the reach of Indian sensitivity. Though the song of the glory of India's past continued, but now with a new note, a note of confidence in the victory of the cause of ordinary workers and peasants.

In the throbbing working class centre of Kanpur amidst the vast Hindi region, there rose a new generation of poets and writers who, inspired by the Great October Revolution, attacked the exploiters and attempted to fill the people with hope of a new type of liberation that would put political power in the hands of the working people. They all clustered around poet 'Sanchi' (whose militant pen name was also Trishul, the trident, weapon of the god of destruction, Lord Shiva) and his magazine Sakavi.

The other rallying points of new rebel poets and writers were the magazines *Pratap* edited by the great patriot and prose writer Ganesh Shanker Vidyarthi and *Prabha* (Khandwa in MP) of the equally great patriot and poet, Makhanlal Chaturvedi. These poets were joined by Navin, Dinkar, Subhadra Kumari Chauhan and others.

All these writers were inspired by the socialist ideas that every man and woman should be equal and fruits of labour should also be enjoyed equally by all. Sanchi said in his poem "Communism" (written on April 12, 1920):

> Some people are starving, bodies losing all blood and flesh. While some have eaten so much that they suffer stomach ailments. In floods of the rivers of equality now all the differences of the high and the low would be swept and like water everything would be levelled.

That was the period when militant nationalism asserted and affected the writers. Navin and Dinkar later swore by Gandhism (mainly after independence), but in their pre-1942 works, they called for militant and even armed struggle against imperialism and for the rights of the working people. They then castigated the philosophy of non-violence.

Dinkar specified the October Revolution as: "the spark of Lenin's heart" and wished in many other poems that India could undergo such a violent shake-up. Later, when he differed with the Indian communists, he did not forget to remind that he still worshipped the Kranti Bhawani (goddess of revolution) and wished that communists would take a leading part in the struggle for emancipation.

Towering Part

The towering part of that whole creative process of the revolutionary realism consisted of the works of Munshi Premchand. He unravelled the feudal and colonial oppression and the rising capitalist class in league with the feudal elements in his short stories and novels. Those themes found their pinnacle in one of his last works, novel *Godan.*

Another fiction writer worth remembering was 'Ugra' who attacked conservatism, superstition, feudal and religious hypocrisy, pretending socialists, etc., generally blended with satire, hitting sometimes below the belt that earned the applause of the then new radical generation.

Much of the prose writings of the great poet, 'Nirala' and also some of his poems, did bear these characteristics.

These rebel tendencies appeared quite powerfully in the first collection of short stories, *Angaare* (Embers), of Marxist writers, Sajjad Zaheer, Ahmed Ali, Dr. Rashid Jahan and Mahmuduzzafar, who later founded the progressive writers movement under the chairmanship of Munshi Premchand. The collection was, however, in truly Ugraian fashion, not Premchandian.

In the organised progressive writers movement, Marxism and the October Revolution emerged as the most important factors in literary ideology. The Soviet Union stood as the embodiment of the practice of socialism. The top Chhayavadi (The romanticists who began to assert liberation of forms in poetry and emphasised highly expressive words for creation of the most sensitive poetry). Poet Sumitranandan Pant declared the end of an era in Hindi literature and heralded the beginning of a people's culture in two of his collection of poems, Yugani (end of an era) and Gramya (rural damsel). In one of his poems, he paid tributes to the Soviet Union in the following words:

> Crossing the sea of blood, playing dangerously with embers,
> Jumping over the steep mountains of obstacles and barriers,
> Came up the horizon of revolutions, the dawn of a new age,
> Throbbing in the earth and people's heart, with the welfare of men,
> The prosperity and the beauty of life after building bridges,
> Among the peoples, exiting helplessness and misery
> And driving away from the entire earth the devil of inequality

The progressive tendencies dominated the literary scene to such an extent that a non-Marxist literary critic, Nandadularay Vajpai, said in 1940 from a non-Marxist forum:

> Where is the field of best literary creations today? Undoubtedly, in the field of socialist ideas. Why? Because it is this field that attracted the best from amongst the new talents. How is it, the current religious fields have not become the breeding ground for best literary works and aesthetic art? Why are they satisfied with copying the old or with borrowing progressive styles from new fields of creation?

Here, we must remember the great writer and thinker, Rahul Sankrityayan, who contributed most in popularising Marxism, in fighting out the conservative social idea and in interpreting old heritage from the people's angle.

Poet Nirala, after initial hesitations, also plunged in the progressive writers movement in the last part of his life and gave a new vitality and idiom to the progressive poetry.

By the 1940s, a new generation of writers and poets had emerged; among them were Bachchan, Narendra Sharma, Anchal, Girija Kumar Mathur, Muktibodh, Sheel, Nagarjun, Kedar, Shamsher, Trilochan, Virendra Misra, Shivmangal Singh Suman, J.P. Milind and others who had one thing in common: their active participation in the anti-fascist struggle, the fight against Bengal famine and the revolt of Indian naval forces in 1946 in which the guns could not open their mouths in the Aurora style that heralded the Great October, perhaps, for lack of leadership.

Narendra Sharma, Suman, Anchal and Virendra Misra were the most popular poets of that period (1942-1946). Among the fiction writers the lead was taken by Amritlal Nagar, Upendranath 'Ashk', Nagarjun and others.

In that period, there were a spate of writers' anti-fascist conferences and almost a flood of anti-fascist songs and plays. Narendra Sharma exhorted the people:

> Enemy of the Red Russia is enemy of all people,
> Specially of all workers and all peasants.

Suman's lines "Ten weeks became ten years, Moscow is still far away" were known to the entire Hindi speaking population.

The post-war generation of our writers has celebrated every success of the socialist state of Soviet Union and specially concentrated too castigate the war-mongers, the US imperialism, and their atomic power. Dhoomil, Vijendra, Kumarendra, Leeladhar Jagudi, Som Dutt, Arun Kamal and host of other young writers have contributed to the strengthening of peace-movement and anti-imperialists.

And last but not the least is the folk and mass poetry movement that grew up with the progressive writers movement Rambilas Sharma, Shailendra, Sudarshan, Man Singh Rahi, Khem Singh Nagar, Sahib Singh Mehra, Ramker and thousands of others were inspired by the Great October Revolution and took its revolutionary message to the people in their language and idiom.

The manifestation of the Great October Revolution should not be merely seen in poems or prose written directly about it; it should be seen in the broadening of humanist horizon, sharpening of perception of injustice, deepening of the spirit of revolt and democratisation, of forms of literary expression. Now the dawns and dusks, the flora and fauna, seasons, seas, mountain and rivers and every word meant something more significance than being a thing of beauty.

This small note should be sufficient to show that during the last seventy years, the influence of the Great October has been all-pervading and multi-dimensional that left an indelible mark on literary history.

(*New Age Weekly*, November 8, 1987)

Poster of the movie "Dharti Ke Lal" directed by K.A. Abbas. The film was made by IPTA in 1946. It was based on the famous play 'Nabanna' by Bijon Bhattacharya and 'Annadata', story by Krishna Chander. The film had music by Ravi Shankar and lyrics by Ali Sardar Jafri and Prem Dhawan. The film was based on the Bengal famine which killed millions.

A Supplementary Note on Progressive Cultural Movement

After the revolution in Russia, care was taken by leaders and guards of the revolution to build and develop a new culture which would reflect socialist values. This is to underline here that culture is not limited to production of arts, but how people interact with each other, how they work, celebrate, entertain, mourn, live etc. Lenin himself endorsed Pushkin, Gogol, Tolstoy, Gorky and many others' literature as heritage. It was not mere praise but a scientific critical appreciation. At that time, in many Russian provinces literacy rates were as low as 2 per cent and many did not have their own script. Within 30 years of revolution, they turned the entire population not only literate but educated and skilled. With limited resources, the best of films were produced in USSR. The concept of class in music was thoroughly discussed and a new kind of music was created. In other cultural expressions like sports, USSR excelled, the remnants of that can still be seen. Gorky's "Mother" became the mother of working people in every country. The October Revolution influenced the aesthetics of every single art form and above all the day-to-day lives of the common people.

When the message and ideals of the October Revolution reached India, it brought changes in content, subject, form and readership in the literary world and contributed to the process of decolonisation of cultural space. There were already pro-people themes and leanings in Indian art forms. Writers like Bhartendu Harishchandra, Bhikhari Thakur, Fakir Mohan Senapati etc. picked up non-elite themes. Artists across India greeted the ideals of Equality, Fraternity and Justice. The ideals of the October Revolution helped Indian artists to identify the true nature of British rule which was exploitative. Hence, it is not surprising that in Tamil, Subramania Bharti greeted the October Revolution and M. Singaravelu Chettiar in Tamil Nadu celebrated the first May Day in India. In Hindi, Premchand, Rahul Sankrityayan and many others embraced socialism and adopted scientific socialism in their writings. In Bengali, Jeevananand Das and other poets, in Malayalam, Kumaran Asan and others celebrated the new dignified human. Inspired by the Russian Revolution a novel titled 'Malapalli' was written in 1920 in Telugu by Unnava Laxminarayana. The most revered literary figure of Urdu language, Allama Iqbal who was not a Marxist, also hailed the Russian Revolution. Hasrat Mohani and Sajjad Zaheer pioneered socialist ideas in Urdu. A fresh wave of new writers came who were directly taking their literary ideas from the October Revolution. Later, Ali Sardar Jafri, Faiz Ahmad Faiz, Krishan Chandar, Rajinder Singh Bedi, Manto, Khwaja Ahmad Abbas, Vamik Jaunpuri, Jaan Nisar Akhtar, Majaz Lakhnawi, Makhdoom Mohiuddin, Kaifi Ajami, Dr. Rasheed Jahan, Razia Sajjad Zaheer, Ismat Chughtai, and many others wrote directly about the struggles of the common people, socialism and internationalism.

The ideas of class and inequality penetrated deep in all Indian languages, even in some dialects as reflected in Awadhi poetry by Balabhadra Dikshit 'Padhees'.

In the wake of fascism, socialism also brought writers and artists together through the Progressive Writers' Association (PWA) in 1936 and the Indian People's Theatre Association (IPTA) in 1943. PWA heralded a new era of resistance and gave a vast platform to writers transcending languages and regions. The best of writers from every language got associated with it. These two organisations put the socialist values on top in their respective organisational constitutions.

IPTA was founded under the chairmanship of Prof. Hiren Mukherjee and with guidance from P.C. Joshi. It was none other than scientist Homi Jehangir Bhabha who gave this name to IPTA. It was the same time when almost three million people died in Bengal because of the man made famine. These lives were of no concern for British rulers. Indian hoarders were making profit from the famine. P.C. Joshi asked the artists to go to the villages of Bengal, help party people in running community kitchens and make the villagers understand through their art that it is not fate but the exploitative policies of the capitalist-colonial rulers which had brought this calamity upon them. On the other hand, he suggested to the artists to go to the rest of India and tell the story through plays and songs of the starving and dying people of Bengal and expose the nexus of Indian capitalists and British rulers. Based on this theme, a play was written by Bijon Bhattacharya and Shombhu Mitra directed the play. Vamik Jaunpuri wrote songs for it. IPTA formed a central troop and traveled across the country with this play and collected contributions for famine survivors. It brought immense popularity to IPTA. IPTA ventured into film making also with 'Dharti ke Lal' directed by Khwaja Ahmad Abbas. Balraj Sahni, Shombhu Mitra and many others acted in it. The scenes of migrating farmers were filmed with the help of All India Kisan Sabha members. The direct influence of the Russian Revolution was evident in the film when it talked about the collectivisation of agricultural land and resources as the only possible resolution of the crisis Bengal peasants were facing.

The October Revolution brought a paradigm shift in all art forms which can be seen in the paintings of Chittoprasad, in the sculptures of Ramkinkar Baij, in the dance of Uday Shankar, in the photographs of Sunil Janah. Indian cinema was widely influenced by socialist ideas and movies like Dharti Ke Lal, Neecha Nagar and Garam Hawa were made. Directors like Ritwik Ghatak and K.A. Abbas depicted class consciousness on celluloid and a new realist cinema emerged.

IPTA brought a qualitative shift in Indian theatre. Actors like Prithviraj Kapoor, Balraj Sahni, directors like Shombhu Mitra and Habeeb Tanveer, musicians like Salil Chowdhary and lyricist like Shailendra and Sahir Ludhianavi were associated with it. It aroused Indian masses against inequality and exploitation and lived up to its motto – "People's Theatre Stars the People". They tried to create a culture reflecting the high values of socialism. In a caste ridden, feudal society like ours it was not easy to translate the ideals of equality and egalitarianism into art forms. Writers and artists were committed to the broader goals of socialism and they created new kinds of art – art of and for the masses. They broke the largely elitist monopoly of readership and content. The progressive artists showed the decadent societal structure, its inequalities and with it, the hope for a new future, a new human. The IPTA teams used to perform their shows in working class colonies in coordination with the trade unions. Many famous personalities of that time used to go, watch, sometimes participate and appreciate these performances. When Balraj Sahni was organising IPTA in Mumbai, he discovered many great talented poets and singers living in slums and textile mill workers colonies. He discovered Anna Bhau Sathe, Lok Shayar Amar Sheikh, Gavankar Buwa, and many such artists, who were writing revolutionary songs with modern thought and sensibility using the traditional or folk style.

The stream of revolutionary thought and socialist ideology remained dominant in the field of literature and other art forms. Truly, as Premchand called, the norms of aesthetics of various art forms changed and changed for the better. However, it remained confined to the art forms. The culture of the people, which is not merely art, includes their way of life, their value systems, their behaviour with others and their world outlook, etc. The progressive and scientific cultural values did not penetrate that deep into the lives of common people where it could uproot feudal as well as colonial culture from their mindset.

While continuing the process of decolonisation one has to keep in mind the complex realities of society and simultaneously combat any attempt of revivalism. It is a multi-faceted and complex process. The post-independence leadership of India succeeded only marginally in achieving that end. Still, the cultural movement began by people influenced by the values of socialism, continued and even today theatre and literature largely carry anti-communal, anti-caste, pro-downtrodden contents.

New Russia

Subramania Bharti

The mighty Goddess of power
looked pleasantly towards Russia —
Revolution that ushered a new age there
With anguished cry, the oppressors have collapsed there
Gods are jubilant, with happiness and pride
While forces of evil are behind and listless.
Oh! People of the world, look, look well at this unique new
All of a sudden everything is changed
Laws are being enacted for the welfare of the men.
In order to awaken the world, they cry out;
There is the Raj of all mankind
There are no slaves anymore, nor illgotten wealth from slavery
Like a shattered wall, the present age lies on the ground
The golden age is about to come.

(1917)

13

Message of October Revolution cannot be Blurred

A.B. Bardhan

Eighty six years have passed since that unforgettable day in 1917 when the workers in Russia, together with soldiers in the field (peasants in uniform) carried out the Revolution that overthrew the bourgeois-landlord regime. The decrepit tsarist rule had already collapsed a few months earlier.

Led by Lenin and the Bolshevik Party, the Revolution brought into existence a Workers and Peasants' State – the Union of Soviet Socialist Republics.

The Great October Revolution, as it came to be called, heralded a new era in history. Hitherto, revolutions had replaced one exploiting class or ruling group by another exploiting class or group. This was a revolution that had thrown out the exploiting classes from power in a vast country, and had put the exploited classes in power. For the first time it was shown that the capitalists and landlords or their agents do not have the divine right always to rule and lord over a country and its people. The working people can also rule and manage the affairs of their country, even against overwhelming odds. The age-old myth was smashed.

Just to remind those who might have forgotten or had not heard, the tremendous power and vitality of the Revolution was proved by the fact that the Workers' and Peasants' Red Army which was built up from scratch routed the white bands of professional officers and mercenaries in a brutal civil war, and came out victorious through a war of intervention launched by the imperialist powers from several directions – an operation which Winston Churchill had picturesquely called the "March of Fourteen Armies".

The country lay devastated as a consequence of these wars and the World War that had preceded it. But within less than two and a half decades, backward and ruined Russia literally lifted itself up by its bootstraps to become the world's second most powerful country and economy in the world.

Soviet Union had to fight a war once again. This time the Hitlerite fascists launched a perfidious attack with a massive army backed by the entire resources of Europe. The Soviet Union took on the might of Hitler's army, and routed it at the cost of terrible sacrifices.

In doing so, it rescued the world from fascism. These are historical facts, whose significance cannot be diminished with the passage of time.

The people of the Soviet Union yet again had to engage themselves in the task of rehabilitating and rebuilding their country. This they did. Their technological advance was demonstrated by the fact that they were the first to conquer space. However, as a result of several mistakes and distortions, some carried over from earlier days and some that crept in later, and due to the conspiracies of internal and external foes and the machinations of imperialism, the Soviet Union, ceased to exist by the beginning of the nineties.

There was jubilation in the capitalist world. They celebrated it as the death of socialism and the end of Marxism. They congratulated themselves thinking they had finally exorcised the 'communist evil'. George Bush senior triumphalistically proclaimed the advent of the new 'American Century'. There were those who glibly spoke of the 'end of history', and therefore the eternal rule of capitalism.

Within a decade however, people have begun to witness the bankruptcy of the capitalist order. They are facing the hard truth, that no matter what the so-called new economic policies claim, no matter what 'reforms' are announced and implemented in the name of 'neo-liberalism', capitalism has no solution to the problems of poverty, hunger, unemployment and disease that afflict the overwhelming majority of people and countries. If anything, these problems are getting further aggravated. It is only those who have decided to keep their eyes deliberately shut that cannot see them. People know that the latest advances in Science and Technology are quite capable of raising food production, of producing medicines that can save lives and reduce child mortality, of building schools that can remove illiteracy and raise the cultural level of the masses and of ensuring social security for all. And yet, their potential for serving peoples' needs remains unutilised. They are used only to fill the coffers of the handful of multi-billionaires and the multinationals, for their superprofits.

Marxism-Leninism has always emphasised that it is the people who make history. This truth is becoming self-evident today. People all over the world have begun to understand that the policies of Liberalisation, Privatisation and Globalisation, are nothing but devices for capitalist plunder, for unrestrained exploitation of the world markets and resources, for despoiling nature and the environment. In almost all countries, people are rising up in protest and taking to the streets not in thousands, but in tens of thousands and even hundreds of thousands. They are beginning to mouth anti-capitalist slogans, slogans against imperialist globalisation and so forth. This new rising Peoples' Power will soon begin to make history. Already, this manifestation of peoples' power has brought about revolutionary changes in countries like Brazil, Argentina, Bolivia, and halted counter-revolution in Venezuela. The focus is now on Latin America. It may soon shift elsewhere too. This Peoples' Power has correctly linked the policies of liberalisation, though may be subconsciously, with the policies of imperialist aggression and war.

As early as 1848, when Marx and Engels wrote the Communist Manifesto, they had noted in forceful language the globalising trend of capitalism, 'chasing over the whole surface of the globe', 'nestling everywhere, setting everywhere, establishing connections everywhere, meeting the need of a constantly expanding market'! With scientific precision, they had underlined its consequences for all countries. Lenin carried forward this analysis, in the epoch of imperialism. Since then there has been an unprecedented growth of monopolies, the emergence of multinational corporations based in the developed capitalist countries, and the rise of international Finance Capital criss-crossing national borders everyday, every hour. We see how imperialist globalisation today subordinates the national economies of several countries, dominates the markets of developing countries and intensifies their exploitation manifold. Marxism reveals the historical development of all the features of capitalism in the present era of imperialist globalisation. It also shows how this has to be combated by building the combined resistance and counter-offensive of the people, nationally and internationally.

It is the October Revolution that unfurled the banner of Marxism-Leninism as the ideology of revolutionary change, of emancipation of mankind. The millions who are taking to the streets today may not yet be aware of the road along which they have to travel, and the destination which they have to reach. For that they have to undergo a lot more of experiences. But they will be the subjects of historical change.

It is the October Revolution that carried the ideas of socialism to the remotest corners of the world. It is the gunfire of the October Revolution that woke up the oppressed, the exploited and the deprived from their slumber and urged them to organise and fight to take their destiny in their own hands and shape it. The Soviet

Union may no longer exist. But that has not led and cannot lead to the demise of the great emancipatory ideas that inspired and created it. They continue to live and inspire millions of people in every country.

The French Revolution had been throttled within a few years by the rise of Napoleon Bonaparte who established his empire over virtually the whole of Europe. But the ideas of Liberty, Equality and Fraternity that rose from the barricades in France, continue to ring in the hearts and minds of people everywhere.

The model of socialism that was built in the Soviet Union may have collapsed along with the East European ones that were more

Imperialism today

With the fall of the Soviet Union, began the rise of what is called the "neo-liberal era". Eminent Marxist Prof. Randhir Singh used to say that the Soviet Union had the effect of humanising capitalism. The advanced capitalist countries were forced to take measures to control inequality in their own countries because the Soviet Union served as a model and an idea that challenged the necessity of capitalism. With the rise of neo-liberalism, there was a sharp increase in inequality in both the advanced capitalist countries and the developing countries. It would be a mistake to think that imperialism has ended today because most countries have achieved political independence, or because some sections of the bourgeois in the formerly colonised countries have acquired global power. Rather, the masses of the people in the developing countries continue to be in dire conditions. The Imperialism in our times is openly manifested in the wars in Afghanistan, Iraq, Libya, Syria and Palestine. However, the much acclaimed free market regime contributes to primitive accumulation of capital on a massive scale. Development through dispossession is visible in the entire third world. The working and living conditions of people at large, are at subhuman levels. The global economic elite, though more scattered, remains closely linked to the metropolitan capital of Europe and North America which successfully controls the fate of nations.

or less copies of the first. But the ideas of socialism, of an exploitation-free, oppression-free system are as strong as before. In a number of countries, where the communists are in power – China, Vietnam, Cuba, Democratic Korea, the process of building socialism is going ahead taking the specific characteristics of each country into account.

There can be a flow and ebb in the revolutionary tide. There can be advances and retreats. But Man's endeavour to improve his life, to put an end to exploitation and oppression, to change the world for the better never ceases. And there is no other scientific ideology that shows him the way, other than Marxism.

After an initial set-back, communists the world over are regrouping and carrying on their activities. They are with the people, organising them and leading their struggles. They are meeting and exchanging experiences at regional, national and international levels. Long after the false prophets who gleefully wrote about the fall of the Soviet Union and busied themselves composing books and articles about the alleged crimes and failures committed by Soviet leaders are consigned to oblivion, to the dustbin of history, the October Revolution will continue to inspire ever new generations of revolutionaries. The demise of the Soviet Union has had several negative impacts on world politics. The might of the Soviet Union had a restraining effect on imperialism led by the US, and their threats against developing countries. Its presence had a cooling effect on the hotheads in the capitalist West who planned economic, political and even military aggression against weaker nations. The newly-liberated countries could look to the Soviet Union for moral and material help in facing threats, in undertaking the task of development and thus overcoming the colonial legacy of backwardness.

Among communists and their parties in many countries, the collapse of the Soviet Union initiated a serious discussion and debate about the mistakes and distortions that were committed in the Soviet experiment, which were used by the political conspirators and economic predators for bringing about its fall. Lessons have been learnt.

It has been underlined for the umpteenth time, that Marxism is not a dogma and that socialism is not made according to any cut and dried formula or by copying any model. It is a science that has to develop with the times, with new issues that come up in every field, and which need to be studied and analysed in concrete terms using the tool of dialectical materialism. The materialist conception of history needs to be applied to the specific conditions of each country. Each country has to make its revolution and build socialism in its own way. The countries that are engaged in this task of going forward to socialism, after making their revolutions, are living examples of the concrete application and further enrichment of Marxism.

The message of the October Revolution has not been and cannot be blurred!

Long Live the October Revolution!

(*New Age Weekly*, November 9, 2003)

Fidel Castro (August 13, 1926 – November 26, 2016) and Hugo Chavez (July 28, 1954 – March 5, 2013). Men who carried the legacy of Socialist Revolution to the 21st Century.

14

Revolution that Lit a Great Flame

D. Raja

> Let the ruling classes tremble at a Communistic revolution. The proletarians have nothing to lose but their chains. They have a world to win.

Thus declared Marx and Engels at the end of the *Manifesto of the Communist Party* way back in 1847-48. They explained the history of class struggle dialectically and historically; they proved its inevitability of culminating into a revolution and achieving political power to overthrow all exploitative and oppressive social conditions; such a revolution would lay the foundations for a new civilisation – a socialist society.

The ruling classes in Russia trembled at such a revolution. The revolution succeeded on November 7 (October 25) 1917. It shook the world. Socialism was no more just an idea or an ideal or a utopia. It became real. The idea of Socialism gripped the minds of the people the world over, and became a force to move the people and intensify the class struggle.

Lenin said that "every revolution means a sharp turn in the lives of a vast number of people". Russian Revolution was a sharp turn not only in the lives of Russians or in the lives of people who were under czarist regime. It gave a sharp turn in the lives of people everywhere in the world.

The Russian Revolution paved the way for the toiling people to achieve political power for the first time. Equality, liberty and fraternity could not remain merely abstract human and social values. The triumph of revolution brought radical changes in the psychological frame and social behaviour of human beings with regard to emancipation from all sorts of enslavements and with regard to the questions of equality and social justice.

The Russian Revolution heralded the epoch of the abolition of every kind of exploitation and oppression. The decrees on peace and land signed by Lenin on November 8, 1917 within 24 hours of the success of the revolution were very significant at that point of time. They were:

Decree on Peace called upon all the imperialist and the belligerent governments to end the war. It recognised the rights of the nations of self-determination.

Decree on Land put an end to the monarchy and medievalism, breaking the pernicious feudal structures.

All these proved that socialism really meant to put an end to exploitation of human being by human being and exploitation of nation by nation.

The message of the Russian Revolution moved millions and millions of the people across the world, particularly in the colonised countries. The great strides made by socialist Russia primarily in the social sector and in the social life of the people rattled the imperialist and capitalist countries and forced them to adopt welfare measures and to recognise democratic and other human rights.

The Russian Revolution gave an impetus to the freedom struggles and to the national liberation movements. Finally, colonialism had to collapse and it did collapse. The colonies got liberated. Revolutions advanced in several countries, including in China.

The triumph of revolution and the construction of socialist economy sent shivers down the spines of imperialist and colonial powers. They tried to respond through war and fascism whereby threatening the whole humanity. The young socialist Russia made supreme sacrifices, to defend humanity, in the war thrusted upon them by Hitler and fascist forces. The world was saved from the most reactionary, inhuman and monstrous forces of fascism.

From November 7, 1917 to November 7, 2004 is not a long period in history. But the journey of humanity during this period is one of triumphs and tribulations. A lot of water has flowed in Don and Volga. The Soviet Union disintegrated and the socialist regimes in Eastern Europe collapsed in the 1990s.

Imperialists declared that it was the end of history and end of ideology. They also declared that socialism had no future and Marxism had no relevance. They continue their onslaught against socialism and against revolution through neo-liberal philosophy and economic politics.

Others got confused and tried to revise Marxism and reinterpret revolution. For them, class struggles and revolutions have no meaning. Those who fight against globalisation and for another world are also not clear about the alternative.

The present phase of globalisation is nothing but an imperialist – capitalist globalisation. It has been widening the gulf between the rich and poor within the nation and among the nations. Internet, telecom and mass media cannot wish away the inherent class contradictions that are becoming sharper. The bourgeoisie have no nation and no national interests. Their greed is to have the whole world for making profits. The so called human rights and democratic rights issues are subservient to their pursuit for absolute freedom for their capital to move and to plunder. But the working class and toiling people are chained and subjected to unprecedented neglect and negation of their hard won rights.

The increasing contradictions between labour and capital and the increasing contradictions between the exploiters and the exploited are reflected at national and global levels. Ideology continues to be at the core of these contradictions. The current developments have proved that a setback to socialism in one country, for instance in Russia, cannot be considered a failure of socialism. It is absurd to theorise that socialism has failed and will fail everywhere. Even in Russia, socialism will re-emerge.

The working people of each country will have their own road to socialism, but they will all march forward to realise the human destiny of final liberation. The choice for humanity is socialism and it is the alternative.

In history there are times that not only individuals but political parties, classes and nations can face a situation of "one step forward and two steps back". It is so in the case of the working class and its parties. However, the point is to march forward. As even leaders like Nehru acknowledged, communists have the sense of "marching step by step with history".

Today, we are facing an increase in virulent nationalism from right wing- fascist forces in India. The Soviet experience and the Indian freedom struggle, along with the experience of the Indian communists can help us think of a way forward. The Soviet Union had to deal with the problem of national minorities, eg. Kazaks, Uzbeks, Tartars etc. after the Russian Revolution. Their policy was not to assimilate national minorities into a homogeneous nation but to develop the people of minorities both economically and culturally to a higher level. Their policy stated:

> … in order to overcome the distrust felt by the working masses of the oppressed countries towards the proletariat of states which used to oppress those countries, it is necessary to abolish all and sundry the privileges enjoyed by any national group, and to establish complete equality before the law for all nationalities, and to recognise the right of colonies and subject nations to separation.

Thus, they worked hard to eliminate social differences between different groups but at the same time uplift the language and culture of national minorities.

India also had its own set of internal contradictions which it had to deal with. Tamil Nadu, for example, had a very rigid caste hierarchy at the time of the anti-colonial movement. This led to the formation of the Self-Respect movement by Iyothee Thass Pandit and Periyar which criticised the anti-colonial movement for being dominated by upper-caste ideology and called for social reform. Communist leaders in India, like Singaravelur and Jeevanandham spoke of the need for social reform to work alongside the anti-colonial and anti-imperialist struggle. Singaravelur, born in a fisherman family, looked first towards Buddhism to eradicate untouchability and caste-hierarchy. He eventually became one of the pioneers of the trade union movement in Madras and also participated in the anti-colonial struggle and the Self Respect movement. Jeevanandham participated in the Vaikom Satyagraha but also organised workers in Tamil Nadu after joining the Communist Party. He was also well versed in Tamil literature and used to write poetry and articles on other social issues in Tamil Nadu. Hence his participation in the anti-colonial struggle was not at odds with his pride in Tamil literature. These leaders understood the importance of preservation of minority culture and language, but refused to compromise with imperialism and realised that social reform without an economic agenda would ultimately be futile.

This brings us back to the question of socialism. During the onward march of history towards socialism – a better socialism, the Great October Revolution which lit the bright flame will keep throwing light. It will not remain just a part of history, but a frequent reference to understand the present and move forward with more clarity and confidence. It will continue to be a source of inspiration to all those fighters committed to liberate humanity.

(*New Age Weekly*, November 7, 2004)

The great experiment is still going on with increasing success in modifying the lives of Russian people. By communalising public services for the common benefit, the great difference that exists in other states of the world in the economic conditions of the people has been obliterated. All national resources have been placed for the benefit of the whole community. The cruel difference between the rich and the poor, the worker and the lazy, the master and servant, the over fed and the hungry, the haves and have nots, have been removed from the social economy of the Russian people. The effect of modifying the economic inequality of the various classes and interests in Russia through Communism is seen in the foreign relations of the Russian people.... The spectre of the empire, which haunts the rulers of other lands, has been exorcised from the Russian national mind. The subjugation of the nationality under another is deemed by the Russians as wicked and unholy. A score of states which were once under the hegemony of the Czar, from Baltic to the Caspian have had their freedom and self determination given and secured for the mere asking. Exploitation of weaker nation by the stronger for material resources of the subject peoples has been condemned by the Russian State. These are the fruits of Communism as seen today in Russia.

(Excerpt of the Presidential Address given by Com. Singaravelur Chettiyar at the founding conference of CPI on 26th December, 1925 in Kanpur)

15

October Revolution: Few Lessons

Shameem Faizee

Marking the centenary of the Great October Socialist Revolution (1917) is also an opportunity to introspect and analyse the global economic, social and political developments since the disintegration of the Soviet Union and collapse of the socialist regimes in eastern Europe. This would enable us to chart out a path to meet the new ideological and theoretical challenges faced by the communists and workers parties world over. To reach any conclusion on the present path, one has to grasp the meaning of the first socialist revolution, the tasks accomplished during the period when Soviet people were building a socialist state as well as the mistakes that were committed.

Let us first have a look on what the Great October Revolution meant for the working people and toiling masses world over.

The Great October Socialist Revolution was a genuine people's revolution under the leadership of the Bolshevik Party led by Comrade Lenin. The greatest social breakthrough of the twentieth century was accomplished and defended in the subsequent period by the overwhelming majority of the working people. It realised the demands of deliverance from imperialist war, transfer of land to the peasants, and control over factories and means of production to the workers and the acceptance of the rights of self-determination of nations. It showed the way for transition to the socialist stage. The October Revolution showed that it is possible for the working class, in alliance with the peasantry, to take power and blaze the trail to socialism, towards social and economic justice and equality.

No other socio-economic experiment in any country has achieved so much in so short a period of time and given impetus and direction to human progress. The path to socialist construction in one country, undertaken by the USSR, converted a backward country into a powerful industrialised state within an incredibly short time, under conditions of isolation and blockade. Socialism in the USSR demonstrated that unemployment, illiteracy, deprivation and disease were not inevitable evils of modern times. They could be eradicated and a large measure of social security could be ensured for the masses. This held out a ray of hope to the world of deprived people. It inspired the working class movement in all countries. It compelled even bourgeois economists and capitalist states to speak out for full employment and social security, and to regard elements of planning and state intervention as necessary components of economic policy. It gave birth to the concept of a welfare state.

Against this brief history of only 74 years of socialism in USSR and the ongoing struggle in some socialist countries, we have the four century old history of capitalism and imperialism. Capitalism put an end to the feudal system and led to a vast increase in the production forces of the society. There was a corresponding advance in the social, political and cultural fields. But this system grew and prospered at the expense of brutal exploitation of its working masses and of numerous colonies, the occupation and despoiling of entire continents, enslavement of blacks and the genocide of indigenous tribes, etc. It is imperialism's greed, its search for market and colonies, its desire of domination that plunged mankind into two

World Wars and innumerable regional and local wars. It is imperialism that unleashed the arms race and drew all others after this mad pursuit.

On the other hand socialism has, from its inception, stood for peace, for liberation and progress.

The Leninist national policy broke up the czarist "prison of nations" and for the first time bestowed upon all nationalities in the former empire, measures of equality. It is this policy which gave scores of primitive ethnic communities a script and a written literature, something they did not have before.

Fraternal socialist help drew the vast Soviet East from darkness of obscurantism into the light of knowledge and development. This was a source of inspiration to all people suffering from colonial and feudal bondage.

It was once again the Soviet Union which contributed the most to save the world from Hitler's fascist domination, at the cost of unparalleled sacrifices and unsurpassable heroism. This paved the way for liberation of colonies in Asia and Africa.

A world without wars and armament was what socialism offered first and continually strived for. It was the socialist countries which have acted as shields for the newly liberated countries against imperialist nuclear blackmail and neo-colonial threats.

Steps to end the atomic monopoly of U.S. imperialism and thus counter its efforts at nuclear blackmail had been initiated soon after the war. Soviet science and technology registered spectacular advance during these decades. The Soviet Union overtook America in space science, power and delivery system, and several other spheres in an incredibly short period. It developed the most numerous scientific and technical personnel compared to other countries.

Socialism, freedom from exploitation and oppression, liberation from imperialist bondage – all these ideas gripped the masses and moved millions in all countries as a result of the Great October Revolution and the undeniable achievements of socialism in the USSR.

It can never be forgotten that the socialist Soviet Union lived through a war of intervention by fourteen imperialist powers soon after its birth. It survived a devastating civil war, aided and abetted by the very same powers. It later withstood and then routed the fascist onslaught precisely because of its political, ideological, social and technological superiority. It twice rebuilt itself from ruin and destruction inflicted upon it within two and half decades. In the midst of its own difficulties, it rendered help and assistance, first to the people fighting for independence from colonial rulers and later to the newly liberated countries and people fighting for social and economic justice.

II

When the epoch-making revolution took place in czarist Russia, India was in the midst of its own struggle for freedom from British colonisers. The victory in 1917 in Russia gave a new impetus and direction to the freedom struggle in India. Not only did the class struggle get sharpened but the ideas of socialism too started echoing. The rise in the working class movement in India led to the formation of the first central trade union organisation, All India Trade Union Congress (AITUC) in 1920. Numerous revolutionary movements cropped up and a number of young revolutionaries took to the path of violence. The colonial rulers and the reactionary forces within the broad National Freedom Movement called it "terrorism". Many of these revolutionaries later came over to the communist movement. Leaders of mainstream freedom struggle also repeatedly referred to the Russian Revolution as the symbol of hope for the oppressed masses of colonies. Some radical leaders made socialism the reference point for development in liberated India. From Gandhi and Tilak to Nehru and Subhash Chandra Bose, everyone supported the Russian Revolution and a socialist society. In this background, the Communist Party of India was formed in December 1925. Emergence of the Soviet Union provided clues to solve the problems that we were facing during the freedom struggle. These problems included the right of national self determination, that the right of the oppressed countries to independence from foreign domination; the right not to be dragged into imperialist wars; the rapid industrial and agricultural development of our backward and poverty stricken country; the abolition of feudal land tenures and the distribution of land to the tillers of the soil; raising people's living standards; the spread of mass education, healthcare and culture. Last but not the least, was the problem (and continues to be even today) of keeping our multilingual, multi-racial and multi-religious country united with the consent of all its people. This was the most important issue during the freedom movement and it remains so even today. The path of development as and when the country achieved independence became the focal point of debate in almost all political formations that had emerged with the spread of freedom the movement. Socialism was most accepted concept.

The ideals of October Revolution became the primary source of inspiration, not only for those who were adopting Marxism-Leninism, but the big segment of our National Freedom Movement including the dominant leadership of the Indian National Congress. Apart from communists, there were socialists and liberal leaders of the INC who started pleading for socialism as the most suitable goal to be pursued after the country attained freedom. This trend helped us even after attaining our freedom in opting for a secular democratic set-up and Constitution. The unhindered support of the Soviet Union to the people fighting for national liberation, particularly the victory over fascism heralded the era of decolonisation. India too attained freedom in 1947.

The Soviet Union provided political and economic assistance to all newly liberated countries that were willing to build their own independent self reliant economy. India was among the countries which received maximum moral and material assistance including financial support from Soviet Union and newly emerged East European Socialist regimes.

Our ruling classes, in the beginning, wanted to opt for a development path in the capitalist frame and depend on assistance from the western capitalist powers, particularly Britain and America. But the assistance from these sources was not without strings. The overwhelming majority of the ruling party was reluctant and hesitant to go for this conditional assistance. Gradually they opted for the fraternal help offered by the Soviet Union and other socialist countries. But this decision was neither spontaneous nor without struggle. The ideological and political struggles on choosing the development paradigm in the first decade of independence have a lot for us to analyse and learn from while deciding our strategy and tactics in the current phase of crisis the country is faced with.

The Soviet Union and other socialist countries helped us to build our own industries in coal, steel, and petroleum, pharmaceutical, medical and such other core sectors. These public sector undertakings were the main sources of our strength by which we could withstand the repeated onslaught of imperialism including the global meltdown caused by the crisis of finance capital in 2008.

These decisions to seek help from Socialist world also helped in taking some very important decisions on land reform, nationalising the core sectors of natural resources like oil and coal, abolition of privy purses of feudal lords and ultimately the nationalisation of banks. The idea of making public sector the determining factor of national economy had general popular support. These progressive measures paved the way for fast development of industries and agriculture.

In the international arena, Soviet help to the newly liberated countries and their assertion against imperialist pressure facilitated the emergence of the Non-Aligned Movement that later developed into a “Third Block”. This Block was basically anti-imperialist. It played a very important role in shaping the world events in the last half of the 20th Century.

III

The disintegration of the Soviet Union and the collapse of socialist regimes in Eastern Europe has created a new situation. The process of introspection and analysis is going on. The World Meetings of the Communist and Workers' Parties have attempted introspection on a continuous basis in the past two and half decades. Certain unanimous conclusions have been reached but the process is to be continued as there are several important aspects, particularly related to democracy and democratic set-up in the socialist system, that need to be deliberated upon. The information and technological revolution has thrown up new ideological and theoretical questions that need to be pondered over.

The Communist Party of India in its fifteenth Congress held in Hyderabad in April 1992 adopted a detailed document on the disintegration of the Soviet Union and collapse of the socialist regimes in Eastern Europe. The document reached certain definite conclusions including the one that reiterated our firm commitment to Marxism-Leninism. It also categorically said that the collapse of the Soviet Union was not the collapse of socialism. It was the collapse of a specific model. It further concluded that no model of socialism could be copied. Every country has to evolve its own model based on geographical, national, ethnic and cultural traditions and other local realities. But this document left out analysing the impact of IT revolution on classes and their consciousness. It needed to be studied more.

If we look at the present realities, certain things are obvious. The rule of finance capital, that Lenin himself had described as the crucial stage of most brutal exploitative capitalist systems, is there to impose its economic and political hegemony world over. The CPI, while analysing the economic crisis of 2008 which was termed Global Meltdown, described it as the "crisis of finance capital and not the cyclic crisis of capitalism". The Political Resolution, adopted by the 21st Congress of the CPI held at Patna in 2012, has said:

The world is in the mire of a serious economic crisis that it has not been witnessed since the early thirties of the last century. It is not the ordinary cyclic crisis of capitalism. It is a crisis of the finance capital that attempted to establish its hegemony on the economic and political system world over. In the wake of the disintegration of the erstwhile Soviet Union and collapse of the socialist regimes in Eastern Europe, it was proclaimed that the days of class struggles were over, history had come to an end and the only path of development was through capitalism that propounded the theory of Globalisation, Liberalisation and Privatisation. What actually was meant by this mantra was a total freedom for maximisation of profit by all means and a licence to loot the natural resources in any part of the world. As finance capital has neither a national character nor a grooming in industrial activity, it was bound to be brutal and inhuman in all its endeavours.

...[A]bsence of a credible alternative is leading to far more rightward shift in the European Union. In a number of countries, particularly in Austria, Finland and Hungary, rightist parties have gained in the recent elections. These rightist forces have launched an offensive against the Left. Hungary has outlawed the Left.

The global economic crisis is affecting countries and people in different regions differently. If Europe is in dire straits by heaping miseries on the people through cuts in pension and wages, reduction in public fund for education and public health, raising of interests on public borrowings, the Arab countries too are in turmoil. The bankruptcy of banks and financial institutions in USA and Europe has dwindled the incomes of Sheikhs and Amirs who are passing on the burden to their own people. Apart from urge for democratic and human rights there are economic reasons for the people's uprising in most of the Arab countries. American imperialists along with their NATO allies are out to exploit the people's uprising to protect their own interests in the Middle East and North Africa. They are adopting different yardsticks keeping in view only their interests. Wherever possible, they want to protect their stooges or maneuver installation of another puppet regime. Libya has already been captured, manipulations are on to install puppet regimes in Egypt and Yemen and repeat Libya in Syria. In Qatar as well as in most of the Gulf countries they are out to protect the ruling monarchies. But the global economic meltdown has started affecting most of these countries and hurting the people there who will be out on the streets more and more.

China, Cuba and Vietnam are adopting their own course to continue efforts to build socialism in the context of a globalised economy.

The DPR of Korea is continuing its efforts for socialist construction in a very difficult situation. The present regime in Laos also intends to follow the path of socialist construction.

All these efforts will become more and more relevant as the global economic crisis gets further deepened and more and more people join the resistance movement and ultimately the struggle for an alternative to the hegemony of finance capital. Finance capital has in its nature to go to any low to maximise profit. Karl Marx, in the first volume of the *Capital* itself has quoted T.J. Dunning, the trade unionist as under:

> Capital eschews no profit, or very small profit, just as Nature was formerly said to abhor a vacuum. With adequate profit, capital is very bold. A certain 10 per cent will ensure its employment anywhere; 20 per cent certain will produce eagerness; 50 per cent positive audacity; 100 per cent will make it ready to trample on all human laws; 300 per cent, and there is not a crime at which it will scruple, nor a risk it will not run, even to the chance of its owner being hanged. If turbulence and strife will bring a profit, it will freely encourage both. Smuggling and the slave-trade have amply proved all that is here stated. (Volume 1, Chapter 31)

With a bid for hegemony of finance capital, the capitalist order is reaching to that barbaric stage.

The international finance capital, from day one of its mission for economic and political hegemony had also seen to it that the ideological opponents of economic neo-liberalism are marginalised in their countries. Much more serious was their bid through several streams of non-governmental organisations (NGOs), financed and encouraged under different covers to hijack the issues that the ideological opponents of neo-liberalism could have used to sharpen the class consciousness of the masses.

Apparently, these NGOs took up the noble 'cause', their campaign to disturb the existing class organisations, both mass and political, that could have better fought on these issues. One needs to adopt a clear and conscious approach to such attempts and foil the greater conspiracy of the international finance capital to blunt the class consciousness of suffering masses and disarm ideologically the real fighters of economic neo-liberalism.

(Some excerpts from the Political Resolution of Patna Congress, 2012)

From what is happening at the moment, certain trends and attempts by the finance capital to impose its political and economic hegemony world over can be identified. It may differ from country to country and region to region, but the basic features are common. Let us list some of them:

- Engineer, encourage and spark conflicts within the country, between the countries and regions but keep the control of finance capital on the natural resources.
- Convert the non-imperialist countries into markets and keep them under the control of the finance capital. WTO and IMF are the main tools of this conspiracy.
- Provoke armed conflicts within the country or with neighbors. It helps to capture the natural resources. Arms race only can help imperialism, particularly the U.S. imperialism to revive the industrial military complex and economy as such.
- Marginalising and setting aside class politics; promoting classless consciousness either through the so-called Non-Governmental Organisations (NGO) or floating political parties that claim to be non-class but ultimately serve the interests of the finance capital. Here the communist and workers parties have to be very cautious.
- Blunt the class consciousness in the nonbourgeois classes. Fracture the working class. The emergence of new segments in the middle classes. Fracturing of classes is a reality that cannot be ignored. Impact of IT has to be studied. It too has caused fractuation in classes.
- Fractuation in classes, blunting of class consciousness and emergence of political forces claiming to be non-class is a big challenge that the communist and working class parties can ignore at their own peril.

All these have played an important role in causing a rightward shift world over. In India we are facing a very serious challenge. The last Congress of the CPI held in 2015 has described the formation of the Narendra Modi government as not to be treated just as replacement of one bourgeois party with another. It has said:

> The advent of the Narendra Modi government as a result of the clear majority for the Bhartiya Janata Party in the Lok Sabha elections marks a definite right-ward shift in politics. As the corporate capital has staked everything for the victory of the BJP-led NDA alliance that was actively and aggressively backed by the RSS, the new government clearly represents the combination of the interests of corporate capital, rightwing ideology coupled with the worst form of majoritarianism and communalism having fascist tendencies.

This government is bent upon reversing everything. In political, economic and Constitutional structural arena it is trying to impose an order that endangers the very secular-democratic fabric of the country. It is paving the way for a fascistic take over. On the economic level it is a government that is serving the interests of the corporate and finance capital, heap the burden on the common people, dismantling the public sector, reversing all the policies that were formulated to help the people. It is allowing unbridled entry of finance capital by liberalising all the restrictive measures including limits on FDI and FII.

So far there has been a consensus in the country on foreign policy. It was of an independent, mostly anti-imperialist non-alignment. Now it is being totally reversed. More and more the country is surrendering to U.S. imperialism and politically and economically aligning with its tools like Japan.

It is sparking conflicts on the basis of religion, caste, ethnicity and linguistic affiliation to impose a fascist rule. Hastening the communal-casteist polarisation is its main political weapon.

This cannot be fought back only on the basis of Left unity. While the Left has to build a much closer unity on economic issues and fight on its own the economic neo-liberalism as most of the other bourgeois political formations have swallowed the prescription of neo-liberalism, it has to go for the broadest possible unity of all secular democratic and left forces to combat the fascist threat.

The CPI has, while sticking to its strategy of building a Left Democratic Alternative based on Left Unity has called for building a Secular Democratic-Left Platform to foil the fascistic offensive. It is neither an electoral platform nor any basis for building a Left Democratic Alternative to usher the country towards a democratic revolution. This is only to stop the immediate onslaught of Fascism.

(Based on a paper presented at the 19th Meeting of the World Communist and Workers Parties held at St. Petersburg (formerly Leningrad) in November 2017).

Introduction to Authors

Rajani Palme Dutt (1896-1974)

R. Palme Dutt was a leading figure and theoretician of the Communist Party of Great Britain. He authored a number of books and contributed immensely towards our understanding of Marxism and class nature of Fascism. His major works include *India Today* (1940) and *Fascism and Social Revolution* (1934).

Prabhat Patnaik (b. 1945)

Prabhat Patnaik is a Marxist economist and a well known political commentator. He retired as a Professor from the Centre for Economic Studies and Planning at Jawaharlal Nehru University. He was the Vice-Chairman of the Kerala State Planning Board.

M.N. Roy (1887-1954)

Manabendra Nath Roy was an Indian revolutionary, radical activist and political theorist, as well as a noted philosopher in the 20th century. Roy helped in the foundation of the Mexican Communist Party and the Communist Party of India.

C. Rajeswara Rao (1914-1994)

Chandra Rajeswara Rao was an Indian freedom fighter and a tall figure of the communist movement in India. He was one of the leaders of the 1946 Telangana Armed Peasant Struggle. He served as General Secretary of CPI from 1964 to 1990. He was awarded the "Order of Lenin" in 1974.

G. Adhikari (1898-1981)

Gangadhar Adhikari was a prominent Marxist scholar and theoretician. A chemical scientist by training, he worked with the best scientists of his time including Max Planck and Albert Einstein. He was arrested in the Meerut Conspiracy Case with other comrades. He remained CPI's Politburo member from 1943-1951. Later, he compiled ten volumes of the *Documents of the Communist Party of India.*

C. Achutha Menon (1913-1991)

Chelat Achutha Menon joined the Communist Party of India through the "Labour Brotherhood" movement in 1941. He spent many years in prison and remained underground while evading arrest. He was the first Finance Minister of the newly carved Kerala state. He later became Chief Minister of Kerala in 1969, serving the office till 1977. His tenure is remembered for starting a number of institutions and development projects in Kerala. He was also a Marxist commentator and translator.

Bijoy Kumar Sinha (1909-1993)

Bijoy Kumar Sinha joined the Hindustan Socialist Republican Association HSRA with Ajoy Ghosh and Batukeshwar Dutt. He was convicted in the Lahore Conspiracy Case along with Bhagat Singh and other comrades. He was also associated with the Delhi Conspiracy Case. He was sentenced to life imprisonment in Cellular Jail, Andaman and was released in 1945.

Hajrah Begum (1910-2003)

Hajrah Begum got attached with Marxist ideology at a time when few women participated in the movement. She was associated with the All India Women's Congress but soon understood the limitations of AIWC and adopted a more scientific and materialistic Marxist line. She was one of the founder members of the National Federation of Indian Women and its first General Secretary during 1954-1965.

Rajeev Saxena

Rajeev Saxena was a well-known Hindi poet and writer. He was the General Secretary of the All-India Progressive Writers Association.

Ajoy Ghosh (1909-1962)

Ajoy Kumar Ghosh was an Indian freedom fighter and prominent leader of the Communist Party of India. He was a member of the Hindustan Socialist Republican Association and was tried in the Lahore Conspiracy Case along with Bhagat Singh and other comrades. He was General Secretary of the

Communist Party of India from 1951 to 1962. He was known for his ideological clarity and exposition of Marxist-Leninist thought.

B.T. Ranadive (1904-1990)

Bhalchandra Triambak Ranadive was active in trade union from the late 1920s. He was associated with the All India Trade Union Congress (AITUC) and Girni Kamgar Union. He was General Secretary of the Communist Party of India from 1948 to 1950. After the split in Indian communist movement, he got associated with Centre of Indian Trade Unions (CITU) and CPI(M) and remained so all his life.

A.B. Bardhan (1924-2016)

Ardhendu Bhushan Bardhan was a freedom fighter, trade union leader and a prominent advocate for left-unity in India. He got associated with AISF in 1940 and was elected as President of Nagpur University Student's Union. He was elected to the Maharashtra State Assembly as an independent candidate in 1957 and was actively involved in the Sanyukt Maharashtra Movement. He became the General Secretary of AITUC in 1994 and later served as the General Secretary of Communist Party of India from 1996 to 2012.

D. Raja (b. 1949)

Doraisamy Raja is National Secretary of the Communist Party of India from 1994. He is a member of the Rajya Sabha from Tamil Nadu. He got associated with the All India Youth Federation in the 1970s and later served as its General Secretary from 1985 to 1990. His writings include *The Dalit Question* and *The Way Forward: Fight Against Unemployment* along with numerous articles in Tamil and English on political and social questions.

Shameem Faizee (b. 1946)

Shameem Faizee joined *Hayat* – the Urdu central party organ as a journalist and consistently worked with party central journals since then. Presently, he is Director of Peoples Publishing House (PPH) and National Secretary of the Communist Party of India. He is one of the founders of INSAF, an organisation for the cause of minorities. He is also associated with the activities of the Progressive Writers' Association and Indian Peoples' Theatre Association.

Joshi-Adhikari Institute of Social Studies

Joshi-Adhikari Institute of Social Studies (JAISS) is a registered institution under the Societies Registration Act, 1860 with registration no. S/16252 of 1985. It is named after two great veterans in the fields of science and humanities, who played seminal roles in the political and social life of the country, Com. P.C. Joshi and Com. Gangadhar Adhikari.

Comrade P.C. Joshi, General Secretary of the Communist Party of India from 1935 till 1947 was a great visionary whose contribution in the building of political, social, cultural and literary movements in the country is unparalleled. He united the scattered groups of communists and moulded them into a national party with a base among the people. He helped build and empower mass organisation of peasants and students in the country. He was the inspiration behind the formation of the Progressive Writer's Association (PWA) and the Indian People's Theatre Association (IPTA). He was a leading initiator in the movement for cultural renaissance in India.

Dr. Gangadhar Adhikari was an internationally renowned physicist, and a student of eminent luminaries like Max Planck and Albert Einstein. Apart from his contribution in the field of science, he dedicated himself to the cause of the Indian National Freedom Movement against British colonial rule and for the nation building activities in a newly independent India.

Comrade Joshi and Comrade Adhikari, together with other colleagues, collaborated in spreading the thought of scientific socialism founded by Marx and Engels, and in building the Indian Communist Movement. It is therefore fitting that an Indian Institute of Social Studies be named after them.

The membership of the institution includes professionals and students from the fields of academics, science, technology, leading persons active in the organisations of the writers, persons active in the field of art and culture, social activists from the movements of women, peasants, workers from industry, agriculture and service sector. Institutions may also be admitted as members of the Institute.

Comrade A.B. Bardhan remained its Chairperson till his last. He was very keen to have a platform like JAISS where activists and academics can interact and enrich mutually. JAISS has published several booklets on socio-political and economic issues. JAISS conducted field surveys also to study the problems faced by marginal and poor farmers in eight states of India. It organises workshops, meetings and seminars on relevant themes.